KU-541-442

' ''. 97 MAD (B)

DATE

HIV in Primary Care

by Dr Sara Madge, Dr Philippa Matthews,
Dr Surinder Singh and Dr Nick Theobald

Medical Foundation for AIDS & Sexual Health
(MedFASH)*

* Registered charity no: 296689

Published by:
Medical Foundation for AIDS & Sexual Health (MedFASH)
BMA House, Tavistock Square, London, WC1H 9JP
© Medical Foundation for AIDS & Sexual Health 2011

Acknowledgements
MedFASH is grateful for advice, support and comments from a wide range of individuals during the development of this booklet, including: Dr Hamish Meldrum, Chairman of Council of the British Medical Association; Dr Ewen Stewart, Dr Philippa James and Dr Neil Lazaro of the Royal College of General Practitioners (RCGP) Sex, Drugs and HIV Group; Professor Brian Gazzard of the Chelsea & Westminster Hospital and Dr John Hughes of the BMA General Practitioners Committee, both serving Trustees of MedFASH.

Thanks are also due to the following for help with drafting and information: Dr Laura Waters of Brighton & Sussex University NHS Trust; Dr Annemiek de Ruiter and Dr Graham Taylor of the British HIV Association; Professor Deenan Pillay of University College London; Dr Dan Clutterbuck, Consultant in genitourinary and HIV medicine, NHS Lothian/NHS Borders; Dr Louise Melvin and Julie Craik of the Faculty of Sexual and Reproductive Healthcare Clinical Effectiveness Unit; Dr Valerie Delpech and Meaghan Kall of the Health Protection Agency. Particular thanks are due to Dr Mark Nelson of the Chelsea & Westminster Hospital and Dr Patrick French of Mortimer Market Centre for technical advice and checking.

Sponsored by Bristol-Myers Squibb (BMS). Printing supported by ViiV Healthcare UK Ltd. Neither BMS nor ViiV have had any editorial input or control over the content of this booklet.

Illustrations and figures are reproduced with the kind permission of Dr Nick Beeching of Royal Liverpool University Hospital, Dr Ben Riley of the RCGP's e-learning for Healthcare programme, Dr Valerie Delpech of the Health Protection Agency, Medical Illustration UK Ltd and the Science Photo Library.

Project management: Russell Fleet, MedFASH Project Manager.
Editing: Ruth Lowbury, MedFASH Chief Executive.
Proofing: Jason Penn, BMA.
Design and layout: Tranter design, www.tranterdesign.com

The authors are credited in alphabetical order. MedFASH would particularly like to thank them all for giving their time and expertise in revising and updating *HIV in Primary Care*.

Cover
© CNRI/Science Photo Library
False colour transmission electron micrograph of human immunodeficiency virus particles inside a stricken T4 lymphocyte, a white blood cell of the immune system.

Foreword

Hamish Meldrum

HIV remains one of the most important communicable diseases in the United Kingdom. Early diagnosis coupled with advancements in antiretroviral therapy have led to a substantial reduction in HIV-related deaths in the UK. However, over a quarter of people with HIV in the UK remain undiagnosed. This figure is particularly sobering in light of the significant links between late diagnosis and morbidity and mortality.

Evidence is clear that early diagnosis has long-term health benefits and allows for cost-effective management of HIV as a long-term condition, preventing expensive and distressing major medical interventions further down the line.

Primary care is in an ideal position to support the drive for early diagnosis of HIV and to facilitate the successful long-term management of HIV. GPs and other primary care health professionals have unique breadth and frequency of contact with patients – many of those diagnosed with HIV will have come into contact with primary care services prior to their diagnosis. GPs play a key role in facilitating a collaborative approach across primary and secondary care, particularly helping patients to navigate through the various specialties and agencies. This booklet is an excellent guide for GPs, practice nurses and primary care teams, providing accessible and comprehensive information about HIV diagnosis and treatment.

An open dialogue about HIV with our patients is crucial for HIV prevention, including the promotion of safer sexual and injecting practices. *HIV in Primary Care* provides valuable guidance about how to promote communication with patients across the primary healthcare team, as well as providing practical advice about how to spot the early signs and symptoms of undiagnosed HIV.

The management of HIV and treatment choices are complex and can seem daunting even to experienced healthcare professionals. This booklet includes practical advice relating to adherence to treatment regimens, the side effects of antiretroviral therapy and possible drug interactions with commonly prescribed medicines, as well as guidance on needlestick injuries, record keeping and other practical policies and procedures.

A diagnosis of HIV has huge ramifications for an individual, and HIV patients learning to live with their condition face particular and significant challenges which need to be dealt with in a sensitive manner. There is a need to acknowledge, for example, how important confidentiality, clear communication and continuity of care are to patients with HIV, and that maintaining a strong doctor-patient relationship is crucial for the successful management of chronic conditions such as HIV.

The BMA supports the Medical Foundation for AIDS & Sexual Health and welcomes this guidance as an important tool in helping to raise awareness and equip primary care professionals to deal with the diagnosis and treatment of HIV.

Dr Hamish Meldrum
Chairman of Council
British Medical Association

Preface

About this booklet

The number of people with HIV infection continues to rise. There is no cure and no vaccine, although current treatments are life-saving. Over a quarter of those with HIV infection in the UK have yet to be diagnosed, even though many will be using primary care and other medical services.

This booklet will provide essential information on HIV for GPs, practice nurses and other members of the primary healthcare team. The booklet provides information on:

- HIV and the consequences of infection
- the clinical diagnosis of HIV in primary care
- HIV testing and prevention strategies in primary care
- the management of those with HIV – with a primary care focus.

Comments about this booklet are welcome, and will inform future editions. Please send them to the Medical Foundation for AIDS & Sexual Health.

About the Medical Foundation for AIDS & Sexual Health (MedFASH)

The Medical Foundation for AIDS & Sexual Health (MedFASH) is an independent charity dedicated to the pursuit of excellence in the healthcare of people affected by HIV, sexually transmitted infections (STIs) and related conditions. Originally established by the British Medical Association, MedFASH has been undertaking a range of projects to support and guide health professionals and policy-makers since 1987.

Recent work includes developing national *Standards for the management of sexually transmitted infections (STIs)* with the British Association for Sexual Health and HIV (BASHH) and the *Tackling HIV Testing* resource pack, designed to support implementation of the *UK National Guidelines for HIV Testing 2008*. In 2007, working with the Royal College of General Practitioners, (RCGP), MedFASH developed the Introductory Certificate in Sexual Health, a course for GPs, practice nurses and other primary care practitioners.

About the authors

Dr Sara Madge MBBS MRCGP works as an associate specialist at the Royal Free Centre for HIV Medicine in London, having worked in HIV/AIDS since 1992. She has a background in general practice.

Dr Philippa Matthews MBBS FRCGP is a GP in King's Cross, London. She is an Honorary Senior Clinical Lecturer at the University of Warwick. She has had an interest in HIV, sexual health and sexual history-taking in primary care for many years, particularly how to teach in a way that effects a change in practice. She is also interested in how best to develop and deliver sexual health services in general practice. She is a clinical advisor to the Sexual Health in Practice (SHIP) scheme and is currently involved in assessing to what degree SHIP teaching increases GP HIV testing rates. She was national Quality and Outcomes Framework (QOF) lead for sexual health from 2007-09. She has edited the e-GP Sexual Health and Contraception Module and the FPA *Handbook of sexual health in primary care*.

Dr Surinder Singh BM MSc FRCGP is a senior lecturer at UCL and a GP with a long-standing interest in HIV and AIDS. He has been a senior partner in a thriving practice in Deptford, London since 1992. He was a member of the original Independent Advisory Group on Sexual Health and HIV, established in 2002 as part of the Government's national strategy for sexual health and HIV in England. Latterly he has been a performance assessor for the GMC. Surinder is an enthusiastic advocate of point-of-care testing for HIV.

Dr Nick Theobald MA MSc MBBS trained in general practice in Bath and Wiltshire and was a GP principal in Swindon for nine years. He is currently associate specialist in HIV/genitourinary medicine at Chelsea and Westminster Hospital and Imperial College, London with responsibility for undergraduate and postgraduate education. He chairs the Sexually Transmitted Infection Foundation (STIF) Course Steering Group for BASHH and has been module editor for the eHIV-STI programme.

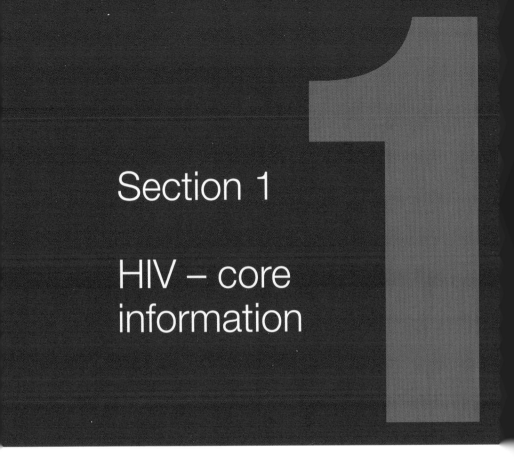

Section 1

HIV – core information

IN THIS SECTION

HIV – core information

For those who need an update on HIV, its effects and how it is treated and prevented.

HIV in the UK: the figures

1. How common is HIV in the UK?

Human immunodeficiency virus (HIV) continues to be one of the most important communicable diseases in the UK, with 86,500 people thought to be infected by the end of 2009. A total of 6,630 persons (4,400 men and 2,230 women) were newly diagnosed with HIV in 2009 (see figure 1).

The annual number of new diagnoses doubled in the first five years of the century and has since declined slightly, with over half (54%) of newly diagnosed individuals infected through heterosexual transmission (see figure 2). The majority of these infections were acquired abroad (see figure 3) and mostly in Sub-Saharan Africa, though this group accounts

Figure 1 | HIV & AIDS diagnoses and deaths in HIV-infected individuals by year in the United Kingdom, 1990-2009

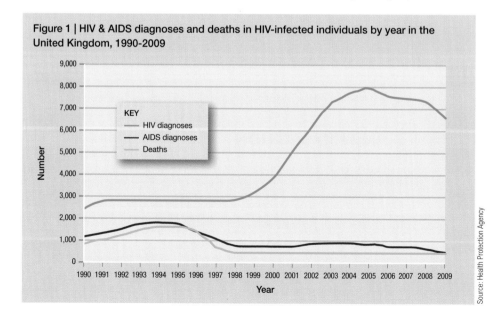

KEY
— HIV diagnoses
— AIDS diagnoses
— Deaths

Source: Health Protection Agency

Figure 2 | New HIV diagnoses in the UK by year of diagnosis and exposure category 1990-2009 (adjusted for late reporting)

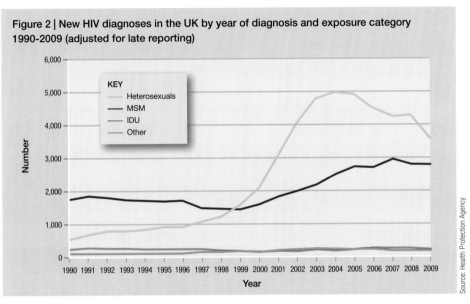

Figure 3 | Heterosexually acquired infection by sub-category of heterosexual exposure, 1990-2009 (observed data unadjusted)

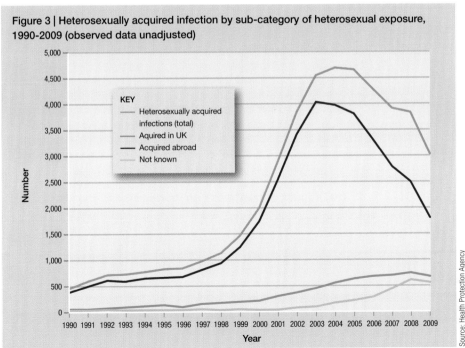

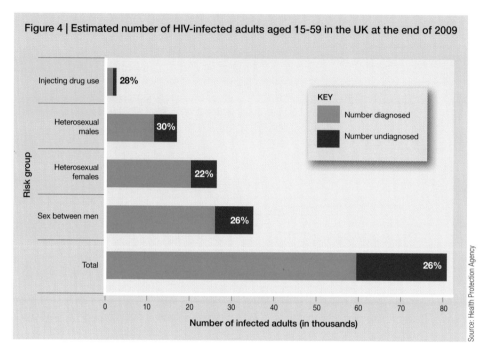

Figure 4 | Estimated number of HIV-infected adults aged 15-59 in the UK at the end of 2009

Source: Health Protection Agency

for most of the recent decline. Of the heterosexuals newly diagnosed in 2009, about a third probably acquired their infection within the UK.

The annual number of new diagnoses in men who have sex with men (MSM) has steadily increased since 2001 from a stable level through the 1990s. It is estimated that four out of five acquired their infection in the UK. There are still high levels of HIV transmission in this group – one in five MSM newly diagnosed has probably become infected within the previous four to five months, according to new research from the Health Protection Agency (HPA).

2. The impact of treatment on death rates in the UK

There has been effective treatment for HIV since the mid 1990s. Antiretroviral therapy (ART) and other interventions have resulted in a dramatic reduction in the number of deaths among those diagnosed with the infection (see figure 1), and for most people it is now a chronic condition rather than an inevitably fatal illness.

3. Undiagnosed HIV

Based on anonymised seroprevalence surveys, it is estimated that over a quarter of people living with HIV (26%, 22,000) remain undiagnosed (see figure 4).

4. Late diagnosis

HIV-related morbidity and mortality are concentrated among those who are diagnosed late. About half of all new HIV diagnoses are made at a stage when ART should already have been started. Although individuals diagnosed late can do well, their life expectancy is reduced and their treatment is likely to be more complex. In 2009, almost three-quarters of UK deaths among people with HIV were in those who had been diagnosed late.

There is evidence that a significant proportion of people diagnosed late with HIV have been seen in general practice within the previous year. Some presented with, in retrospect, HIV-associated symptoms but were not offered an HIV test (see page 97 for a list of indicator diseases).

Early diagnosis improves health outcomes and is also more cost-effective as timely initiation of ART leads to fewer episodes of acute serious illness. ART also lowers infectiousness and the risk of transmission to others.

Monitoring HIV in the UK: how is it done?

1. Measuring diagnosed HIV infection

The HPA and Health Protection Scotland collect information on newly diagnosed HIV infections, AIDS diagnoses and deaths based on voluntary case reporting by laboratories and clinicians. In addition, annual surveys of adults attending for HIV-related care provide a geographical distribution of diagnosed cases as well as information on uptake of antiretroviral therapy.

2. Measuring undiagnosed HIV infection

The Unlinked Anonymous Seroprevalence Surveys provide data on the prevalence of HIV infection in selected adult populations (pregnant women, sexual health clinic attendees and injecting drug users). Blood samples taken in participating centres for other reasons are irreversibly unlinked from patient identifying information and tested anonymously for HIV. The surveys help monitor trends in the prevalence of both diagnosed and undiagnosed HIV infection in these settings. Participants are always offered an HIV test as part of these surveys.

3. Measuring the length of time of infection

New laboratory tests ('incidence tests') are available that are being used in HIV surveillance to help distinguish recent infection (acquired within the last four to five months) from longstanding infection. This surveillance, known as the Recent Infection Testing Algorithm (RITA), is providing useful information on incidence and HIV transmission dynamics at a population level. However, there are currently significant difficulties in interpreting results for individual patients because of confounding factors that can distort the results.

The virus and the natural history of HIV infection

For more on primary HIV infection see page 26

1. The human immunodeficiency virus

HIV is a retrovirus which preferentially infects immune system cells – particularly a class of T lymphocytes called CD4 cells (also known as T helper cells). It is present in an infected person's blood and in other body fluids, including semen, vaginal secretions and breast milk.

A flu-like illness is common in the first few weeks after infection and may be mild or quite severe. During this phase called 'primary HIV infection' (also known as HIV seroconversion illness) there are large amounts of replicating virus and the patient is very infectious.

Once the symptoms of primary HIV infection subside, an asymptomatic stage of infection begins. There are usually no overt clinical signs or symptoms of HIV infection during this stage. There is a wide variation in the time it takes to progress to symptomatic disease and the individual may be well for many years even though the virus is actively replicating. Ultimately the normal levels of CD4 cells can no longer be maintained and as their numbers decline the immune response is undermined.

2. The consequences of HIV infection
Opportunistic infections

For more on clinical problems caused by HIV infection see page 29

If untreated, infection with HIV results in the development of HIV-associated opportunistic infections (OIs). Fungi, viruses, bacteria and other organisms that are usually controlled by a healthy immune system can all cause OIs. Some, such as candidiasis or herpes zoster, are more common in the immunocompromised. Others, such as *Pneumocystis* pneumonia (PCP) only cause infection in the immunocompromised.

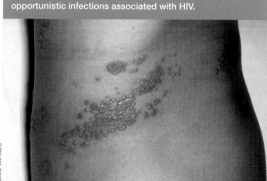

Herpes zoster. Commoner in those who are immunocompromised, this condition is one of the opportunistic infections associated with HIV.

Malignancies

Some malignancies are associated with HIV infection including Kaposi's sarcoma (KS), non-Hodgkin's lymphoma and carcinoma of the cervix. When diagnosed in an HIV-positive patient, these cancers classify the individual as having developed AIDS. Other cancers including cancer of the lung, Hodgkin's lymphoma and some skin cancers may also occur at a higher rate in the HIV-infected patient.

WELLCOME IMAGES

Direct effects
HIV itself causes a flu-like illness in the weeks after infection. In advanced disease it may also cause wasting, diarrhoea and neurological problems, although these may also be caused by OIs.

3. Acquired Immune Deficiency Syndrome (AIDS)
The term AIDS was coined before HIV was identified in order to help classify and monitor a new medical condition. There are now much better measures of disease progression (see pages 17-18) and it is more common to refer to 'advanced HIV disease'. Thus 'AIDS' now has limited value with respect to prognosis. It is, however, still used as a category in epidemiological surveillance and in resource-poor countries.

A patient is said to have AIDS when they develop certain conditions. As well as the malignancies described above, infections leading to an AIDS diagnosis include: *Pneumocystis* pneumonia (PCP), cytomegalovirus (CMV), progressive multifocal leucoencephalopathy (PML), *Mycobacterium avium intracellulare* (MAI), cryptococcosis, cryptosporidiosis and toxoplasma encephalitis.

Tests and clinical markers of HIV infection

1. Combined HIV antibody and P24 antigen tests
The most commonly used test to diagnose HIV looks for both the HIV-1 and HIV-2 antibodies as well as a protein of the virus, the HIV p24 antigen. These 'fourth generation' tests are an improvement on previous HIV tests which looked for antibodies only. The combined test should be available to the majority of GPs in the UK and this can be confirmed with the local lab. In the event of a positive result a second sample is requested for confirmation. The test gives no indication of disease progression.

2. The 'window' period
Antibodies to HIV typically appear four to six weeks after infection, but this may occasionally take as long as 12 weeks. The p24 antigen can be detected in a blood sample within two to five weeks, but it rapidly becomes undetectable once antibodies to HIV start to develop. The period between becoming infected and antibodies developing is commonly referred to as the 'window' period. See box for current British Association for Sexual Health and HIV (BASHH) guidance on interpretation of the combined antibody/antigen tests.

> **USEFUL INFO**
> BASHH Statement on HIV window period, 15 March 2010
>
> - HIV testing using the latest (4th generation) tests is recommended in the BHIVA/BASHH/ BIS *UK National Guidelines for HIV Testing (2008)*. These assays test for HIV antibodies and p24 antigen simultaneously. They will detect the great majority of individuals who have been infected with HIV at one month (four weeks) after specific exposure.
> - Patients attending for HIV testing who identify a specific risk occurring more than four weeks previously, should not be made to wait three months (12 weeks) before HIV testing. They should be offered a 4th generation laboratory HIV test and advised that a negative result at four weeks post exposure is very reassuring/highly likely to exclude HIV infection. An additional HIV test should be offered to all persons at three months (12 weeks) to definitively exclude HIV infection. Patients at lower risk may opt to wait until three months to avoid the need for HIV testing twice.

3. Polymerase chain reaction (PCR) tests

These quantitative assays are a form of Nucleic Acid Amplification Test (NAAT). They are not often used as an initial diagnostic test for HIV in adults as they are expensive and can risk a high false positivity rate in the absence of laboratory interpretation. However, they are now the preferred test used by specialists if primary HIV infection is suspected and the antibody/antigen test is negative.

4. Point-of-care tests

Most point-of-care tests (POCTs) use rapid testing devices which look for antibodies only on oral fluid or pinprick blood samples, and a test result can be given within 15 minutes of the specimen being taken. There are now rapid tests which look for p24 antigen as well as antibodies. The specificity of rapid testing devices is lower than that of standard laboratory tests and, in low prevalence settings, this may result in a significant proportion of positive results being false positives. It is essential that all reactive POCT results are confirmed with a conventional blood test. The use of POCTs should be discussed with your local HIV specialist and virology lab – the validity of the tests in your local area is of paramount importance.

POCTs are useful in situations such as when a sick patient presents to the Emergency Department or a woman of unknown HIV status is in labour. They are also used in community outreach testing and are being used in HIV screening pilots in primary care and acute settings (see page 46).

5. CD4 lymphocyte cell count (CD4 count)

The CD4 count is an indicator of the degree of immunosuppression in those infected with HIV. In healthy, non-HIV-infected individuals the CD4 count is usually above 500 cells/µl, although some have naturally lower CD4 counts. CD4 counts are variable – for example, if someone has a cold or has recently had an immunisation. Overall trends are more important than single readings.

The CD4 count declines at a rate of approximately 40-80 cells/µl per year in untreated individuals with HIV, but some infected individuals progress faster than others. There is wide variation in the time it takes to progress from primary infection to symptomatic disease (see figure 5). Patients with a CD4 count of below 200 cells/µl are at most risk of HIV-related OIs and tumours, but some may not have significant symptoms.

CD4 counts are the main determinant in deciding when to start ART and when to commence prophylaxis against OIs. The table below is a guide showing how CD4 counts can be correlated with the risk of developing particular HIV-related problems – but there will always be some exceptions.

How CD4 counts correlate with HIV-related problems			
CD4 count cells/µl	Risk of opportunistic infection	Risk of HIV-associated tumours	Direct HIV effects
500 and below	Little risk	Hodgkin's disease Cervical cancer	
400 and below	Bacterial skin infections Recurrent bacterial chest infections TB Oropharyngeal candida Fungal infections (skin, feet, nails) Seborrhoeic dermatitis		Lymphadenopathy Sweats
350 and below	Oral hairy leukoplakia Shingles *Pneumocystis* pneumonia Persistent herpes simplex infections	Non-Hodgkin's lymphoma	Weight loss
200 and below	Oesophageal candida Histoplasmosis Cryptococcal meningitis Cerebral toxoplasmosis Cryptosporidiosis	Kaposi's sarcoma	Diarrhoea Wasting
100 and below	Cytomegalovirus infections *Mycobacterium avium intracellulare*	Primary cerebral lymphoma	Dementia

Reproduced with permission from e-GP: e-Learning for General Practice (www.e-GP.org) ©Royal College of General Practitioners 2010.
Opportunistic infection column adapted from: Leake-Date H & Fisher M HIV Infection. In: Whittlesea C & Walker R (eds) (2007) *Clinical Pharmacy and Therapeutics 4th Edition*. Oxford: Churchill Livingstone.

6. Viral load

This is a measure of the amount of HIV in the blood, determined using a PCR test (see page 16), and reflects rates of viral replication. The viral load should fall if ART is acting effectively. A rising viral load in a patient on ART can indicate a range of problems, for example the patient may not be adhering to their regimen or it may be associated with resistance to one or more antiretroviral drugs. Viral load can range from undetectable (defined as the sensitivity of the test – currently less than 50 copies of viral genome/ml of blood) to over a million copies/ml. Numbers of copies/ml are often expressed in a log scale (eg 10^6 copies/ml). The degree of viral replication is linked to the rate of CD4 decline and hence disease progression.

7. How the CD4 count and viral load interrelate

A high viral load predicts a more rapid CD4 decline. The CD4 count of those not taking ART and who have a high viral load is likely to fall more rapidly than that of those with a lower viral load (see figure 5). When the viral load is suppressed CD4 counts recover with a lower risk of developing OIs, tumours and other complications.

Figure 5 | Association between virological, immunological and clinical events, and time course of HIV infection in an untreated individual

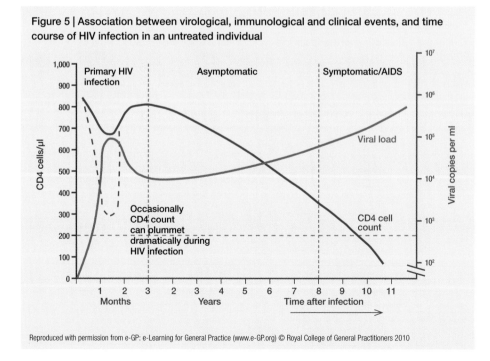

Antiretroviral therapy

Antiretroviral therapy (ART) has had an enormous impact on morbidity and mortality from HIV disease in the UK (see figure 1). New drugs and strategies are continually being developed.

For more on ART and side effects see pages 67-74

The management of HIV has become complex with the advent of ART. This section gives a brief overview of the current specialist management of HIV. For aspects of management that may be encountered by the GP, see the guide to managing HIV-related problems on pages 93-96.

ART limits HIV replication with the aim of reducing viral load to undetectable levels. HIV mutates as it replicates and if drugs are used singly resistance develops rapidly. Therefore, drugs are most often used in combinations of three or more. Adherence to drug regimens is essential.

Antiretroviral drugs are classified into five groups, according to where and how they act in the replication cycle of the virus. They are:
- nucleoside/tide reverse transcriptase inhibitors (NRTIs)
- non-nucleoside reverse transcriptase inhibitors (NNRTIs)
- protease inhibitors (PIs)
- integrase inhibitors (IIs)
- entry inhibitors (EIs).

The effectiveness of ART is monitored by measuring viral load (see page 18). Blood samples can also be tested for drug resistance to help determine the best combination of antiretroviral drugs to use.

After ART has started, drugs may be changed according to any side effects experienced. These can include serious conditions such as hyperlipidaemia, diabetes and lipodystrophy (a syndrome characterised by redistribution of body fat).

HIV prevention in the UK

At a strategic level, efforts to promote sexual health target those in groups associated with a high risk of HIV. It is sensible, for example, to prioritise interventions supporting safer sex with gay men, or projects working on knowledge of HIV and transmission risks among African communities. However, when faced with an individual patient from one of these groups, those working in primary care should make no assumptions about risk.

Each individual's risk needs to be assessed. For more on assessing risk, see page 45.

For more detailed information on sexual history-taking, risk assessment and sexual health promotion, see Sessions 11 001 to 11 003 on www.e-GP.org.uk

1. Promoting safer sexual practices
Penetrative sex
Condom use significantly reduces sexually transmitted infections (STIs) and HIV transmission from both vaginal and anal sex. Condoms should be worn before penetration, and water-based or silicone-based lubricants should be used. Oil-based lubricants degrade latex. Condom failure is more often a function of inadequate lubrication and incorrect fitting than condom thickness. People at risk of acquiring or transmitting HIV should use condoms consistently.

Oral sex

See Department of Health (2006) *Oral sex and transmission of HIV – statement of risk* at www.dh.gov.uk

There is evidence that oral sex, which is common in both heterosexual and homosexual relationships, can allow HIV transmission – especially in the presence of oral disease (ulceration, gingivitis). For a small number of individuals this is the only risk factor in acquiring HIV infection. However, oral sex is very low risk for HIV transmission, especially if ejaculation in the mouth is avoided.

2. Preventing mother-to-child transmission

See BHIVA/CHIVA (2008) *Guidelines for the management of HIV infection in pregnant women* at www.bhiva.org

With appropriate interventions the transmission rate of HIV from mother to baby (vertical transmission) can be reduced to under 1 per cent. Achieving this depends on detecting HIV before pregnancy, or, failing that, in early pregnancy, when the chances of achieving viral suppression by the time of delivery are greatest.

Interventions to prevent vertical transmission include:
- antiretroviral therapy in pregnancy
- antiretroviral treatment at delivery plus a short course for the baby
- elective Caesarian section (although vaginal delivery is an option for women on ART with an undetectable viral load)
- avoidance of breastfeeding.

The ideal time to detect HIV infection is before the woman becomes pregnant. Offering HIV tests routinely to women using contraception – alongside tests for rubella immunity and haemoglobinopathy screens – is good practice, particularly in high prevalence areas. Remember that women may need to be offered further HIV tests if there has been a risk of infection.

See the Infectious Diseases in Pregnancy Screening Programme Standards at http://infectiousdiseases.screening.nhs.uk/standards

All pregnant women should be offered screening for hepatitis B, HIV, rubella susceptibility and syphilis as an integral part of their antenatal care during their first and all subsequent pregnancies.

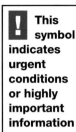

This symbol indicates urgent conditions or highly important information

3. Preventing transmission among injecting drug users

Preventing injecting drug use through education and information strategies is one approach. For those already injecting drugs, there are:

- services that support people trying to quit and that prescribe safer substitutes such as methadone or buprenorphine
- services to support safer injecting practices. Needle exchanges are available in the community where drug users can exchange used needles and syringes for new replacements on an anonymous basis.

4. Risk reduction for people with diagnosed HIV

People with diagnosed HIV infection should follow safer sex and safer drug use practices as described above. For more on sexual and reproductive health issues for people with diagnosed HIV, see Section 3, pages 61-64.

5. Providing post-exposure prophylaxis (PEP): an emergency

PEP is the emergency use of ART to prevent infection when a person has been exposed to a known or high risk of HIV transmission. The aim is to give ART as soon as possible after exposure (within hours, to a maximum of 72 hours). The exact choice of drug combination requires expert guidance. The medication, usually taken for four weeks, can have significant side effects and many people are unable to continue working while taking it.

For PEP following occupational exposure see page 87

PEP may be appropriate:

- following occupational exposure – see page 87 for management of needlestick injuries and PEP
- when an uninfected individual has had sex without a condom with a sexual partner known to have HIV or following sexual assault – see page 81 for post-exposure prophylaxis following sexual exposure (PEPSE).

6. Screening blood and treating blood products

All blood donations in the UK have routinely been screened for HIV since 1985. All blood products in the UK are heat-treated to destroy HIV and other blood-borne viruses.

7. Immunisation

There is little prospect for an effective vaccine against HIV in the near future.

Section 2

How to diagnose HIV in primary care

IN THIS SECTION

How to diagnose HIV in primary care

People who are unaware that they have HIV are attending primary care. Which symptoms and conditions may be clues to HIV infection? How should HIV testing be approached in primary care?

Opportunities to diagnose HIV in primary care

There are two circumstances which provide valuable opportunities to diagnose HIV infection in primary care:

- when the patient presents with symptoms or medical conditions possibly associated with HIV – this is discussed in the first part of this section

> See the *UK National Guidelines for HIV Testing 2008* at www.bhiva.org, www.bashh.org and www.britishinfection.org

- offering an HIV test to an asymptomatic patient because they are or may be at risk of HIV infection – this is included in the second part of this section.

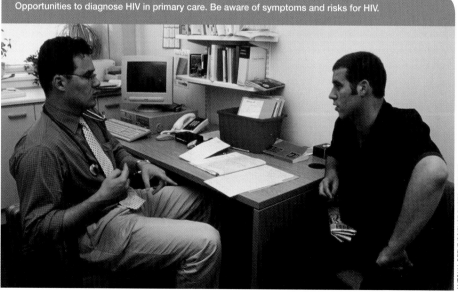

Opportunities to diagnose HIV in primary care. Be aware of symptoms and risks for HIV.

ANTONIA REEVE/SCIENCE PHOTO LIBRARY

Talking to patients about HIV

This may be challenging to the clinician, especially if raising the subject with someone who is not expecting it. In this section we suggest verbal strategies that may be used in a variety of clinical situations. These are indicated in the speech bubbles on pages 47-49.

There are three important principles

Be open with the patient about the clinical reasoning behind your questions

A patient with a skin rash who is suddenly asked 'Can I ask if you are gay?' will wonder what the doctor is up to and, if he is gay, whether it is wise to answer honestly. If the doctor first lays out the clinical grounds for asking the question, the patient may be better prepared to give a full history. There are examples of how to do this later in the booklet.

Be non-judgemental

It is advisable to be direct but sensitive in your questioning. The more accessible and understanding you appear, the more trusting the patient will be, and the more accurate the replies. If the patient perceives the clinician to be disapproving or judgemental, they will be more likely to withhold information and may not return for future care and follow-up.

Ensure your service is (and is seen to be) confidential

Patients may have concerns about confidentiality, in primary care in particular. This may inhibit open discussion of personal issues. Ensure your practice develops a confidentiality policy and implements it through training and induction. Let your patients know that the policy is in place by displaying a confidentiality statement.

For practice policies and systems see page 84

The clinical diagnosis of HIV

There is evidence that a significant proportion of people who present late with HIV infection have been in contact with doctors in preceding years with symptoms which, in retrospect, were related to HIV. Late diagnosis of HIV infection contributes substantially to morbidity and mortality. More advanced disease leaves people vulnerable to overwhelming infection until their CD4 count has risen in response to treatment.

The clinical diagnosis of HIV-related conditions in primary care is not always easy. Many problems associated with HIV are commonly seen in people without HIV infection, for example, seborrhoeic dermatitis, shingles, folliculitis or a glandular fever-like illness. It barely seems feasible to consider HIV first – and then to raise it – whenever common conditions such as these present in the surgery.

Nevertheless, the GP is familiar with the concept of considering rare but serious conditions when extremely common symptoms present. We make quick assessments to answer questions such as 'Could this febrile child have meningitis?' or 'Could this headache be due to a brain tumour?' In this section we try to give the GP a realistic and pragmatic approach to improving their chances of detecting HIV infection.

There are two main clinical opportunities for diagnosing symptomatic HIV infection in primary care:
- primary HIV infection
- conditions associated with longstanding HIV infection.
  These are dealt with in turn.

Primary HIV infection

Primary HIV infection (PHI – also known as seroconversion illness) occurs soon after infection – usually between two and six weeks.

IMPORTANT!
An HIV test is likely to be positive in primary infection, but it may be negative (see page 27). If in doubt, re-test in a week.

Symptoms develop in over 60 per cent of people at this stage. They may be mild and non-specific, but can also be marked and precipitate a consultation with the GP and, occasionally, hospital admission. Even a very HIV-aware doctor is likely to miss some patients with PHI.

Diagnosis of primary HIV infection is valuable because:
- the next opportunity for diagnosis may be at a late stage of disease progression, and so the prognosis for the patient is likely to be much worse
- identifying the infection may protect others from becoming infected.

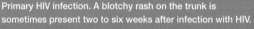
Primary HIV infection. A blotchy rash on the trunk is sometimes present two to six weeks after infection with HIV.

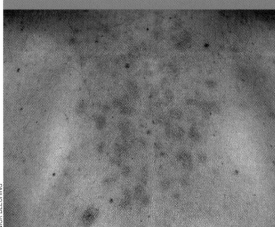

NICK BEECHING

Symptoms and signs of PHI
The patient may have none, some or all of these:
- fever
- sore throat
- malaise/lethargy
- arthralgia and myalgia
- lymphadenopathy.
  If you are thinking of glandular fever, remember to consider primary HIV infection.

Symptoms and signs that are sometimes present and are more specific to PHI include:
- a blotchy rash affecting the trunk
- orogenital or perianal ulceration.

Other features that are less commonly present include:
- headache or meningism
- diarrhoea.

The CD4 count may drop acutely (albeit temporarily) at this stage of HIV infection, and so acute conditions associated with immunosuppression may also occur, including:
- oral candidiasis
- shingles
- other conditions associated with immunodeficiency (see pages 29-38).

What to do if you suspect primary HIV infection

Nothing is going to make this an easy consultation. As the symptoms can resolve within three weeks, you will need to act quickly if you think the patient has PHI.

1. Take a history and conduct an examination to look for further evidence of PHI. Has the person had a rash? Or sores or ulcers in the mouth or genital area?

2. If you remain concerned, raise it with the patient. "Illnesses like this are usually caused by viruses, for example the glandular fever or flu virus. Some quite rare viruses can also be a cause, and it is important that I don't miss them if they occur. I don't know if you are at risk, but HIV is one of these." Assess risks within the last 12 weeks. "Could I ask you a few questions to see if you could be at risk?"

3. If the patient has an identified risk for HIV or they have other clinical features of PHI, do the test and offer safer sex advice at this point. The result will be back in about a week so make an appointment for them to attend.

4. If the result is positive, arrange referral to HIV specialist services. If negative, retest (one week after the first test), reiterating the safer sex advice.

For more on assessing risk see page 45

5. If the second result is negative, this is highly likely to exclude PHI.

case study

A man with a flu-like illness

Ian, a 28-year-old white British male, had been registered with the practice two years, but had only attended once before, for smoking cessation advice. He attended his GP saying he had flu and felt dreadful. He said he was exhausted and was now in the eighth day of his illness. He had a sore throat, ached all over and felt feverish.

It was the severity and duration of the symptoms that made the GP consider glandular fever and HIV. First, she asked Ian about rashes (he had none) and oral and genital ulceration. Ian said he had mouth ulcers. On examination the GP could see three.

After discussing glandular fever, the GP raised the subject of HIV and explained that very rarely an illness like this might be caused in the early weeks of HIV infection. The GP took a partner history and established that Ian lived with his male partner, a relationship of six years. Ian indicated that he felt that his relationship was mutually monogamous. There was no history of drug use.

The discussion appeared to make Ian anxious, so the GP said: 'On the basis of what you have told me your illness is unlikely to be primary HIV infection.' She asked Ian if he would be interested in having an HIV test 'in any case' and he said he would consider it. Ian returned within a week and explained that he had had unprotected sex five weeks before with a new partner he had met in a club. He had now discussed the situation fully with his partner at home, and had decided to have a test. Having spoken to an on-call microbiologist, the GP was aware that the local lab offered combined antigen/antibody tests as standard. She took a sample and the test was found to be HIV p24 antigen positive, but antibody negative, confirming primary HIV infection. Ian was initially distressed and overwhelmed by feelings of guilt. Hospital follow-up was arranged.

Ian's long-term partner, Will, was also registered with the practice. The couple were seen together and it was established that they had had one episode of unprotected sex between the time Ian had contracted the infection and the time he initially saw the GP. Then they didn't have sex until some time after HIV infection was confirmed. Will tested negative both initially and three months later. Six months after this the relationship had survived and the couple were continuing to practice safer sex. Ian was optimistic and had returned to work. The couple told the GP that they felt that Will had been saved from getting HIV because she had been 'so on the ball'.

Learning points

- Some men who have sex with men may initially not volunteer – or be reluctant to disclose – information about their sexual life.
- General practice is well placed to support the partners of HIV-positive people.
- Sexual partners of anyone diagnosed with HIV should be offered an HIV test as routine.

> It was the severity and duration of the symptoms that made the GP consider glandular fever and HIV. First, she asked Ian about rashes (he had none) and oral and genital ulceration. Ian said he had mouth ulcers. On examination the GP could see three.

Clinical conditions associated with longstanding HIV infection

Problems associated with HIV infection may be subtle and insidious, and patients may recover and be well for some time before encountering another problem. Subtle symptoms may mask serious illness, and conditions GPs may have been trained to think were harmless may indicate HIV disease.

IMPORTANT!

Don't miss urgent or life-threatening conditions. Don't miss PCP!

Memorise the conditions in this section that are highlighted as urgent by the symbol above.

Most serious problems usually occur at very low CD4 counts (below 100) so other clinical clues to immunosuppression are likely to be present.

Pneumocystis pneumonia (PCP) is an exception to this rule as it tends to occur at higher CD4 counts (below 200). It may be the first HIV-related problem for which the patient seeks advice. The prognosis correlates directly with how early or late the infection is identified and treated: PCP can kill if diagnosed too late.

When you encounter any of the conditions given in this section, allow the thought of HIV to go through your mind. The stakes are high for these patients – HIV diagnosis at this presentation may be life-saving. The possibility of immunosuppression is especially important to explore if:
- the patient has had more than one of the conditions listed below in the preceding two or three years; or
- the patient has had unusually severe or difficult to treat forms of the conditions listed below.

There are many examples of patients being referred to secondary care with these symptoms without being tested for HIV. This delays diagnosis and wastes time and money with patients attending general medical outpatient clinics for expensive (and frequently irrelevant) investigations. It may also put others at risk of acquiring HIV.

For table of clinical indicator conditions see page 98

Guidance for assessing problems that may be HIV-related
- **Enquire** about weight loss, sweats, diarrhoea
- **Examine** the patient for other signs of immunosuppression (mouth, skin and nodes)
- **Review** the records for evidence of HIV-associated problems (see list pages 30-38)
- **Discuss** the possibility of HIV with the patient to consider their risk
- **Decide** on priorities: is urgent assessment by a specialist required or can an HIV test be offered?

Mouth, skin and nodes see pages 35-37

Think HIV and be prepared to offer the test – don't assume someone else will do it!

The *UK National Guidelines for HIV Testing 2008* contain tables of clinical indicator diseases for adult and paediatric HIV infection. They list conditions that are AIDS-defining in the patient who is known to be HIV-positive; in patients whose HIV status is unknown these are indicator conditions and should usually prompt the offer of an HIV test. The tables are reproduced at the end of this booklet in the Quick reference section. Where conditions listed in the table are mentioned in this section, this is highlighted in a 'Guidelines recommend' box.

1. Respiratory conditions

Cough, sweats, shortness of breath and weight loss may be caused by several opportunistic infections, including community-acquired bacterial infections. *Pneumocystis* pneumonia (PCP) is the most important infection not to miss in the short term. TB is also important. Occasionally, lymphomas or Kaposi's sarcoma may affect the lungs in HIV-infected patients.

PCP
This is a life-threatening infection with symptoms which often have an insidious onset progressing over several weeks. Arguably, PCP is the single most dangerous trap for the unwary GP as it may be the first HIV-related clinical problem the patient has. The prognosis correlates directly with how early or late the infection is identified and treated: PCP can kill if diagnosed late.

Symptoms
- a persistent dry cough of a few weeks' duration
- increasing shortness of breath or decreasing exercise tolerance (clinicians should ask because patients may not mention it)
- difficulty in taking a full breath (this reflects loss of elasticity of the lung tissue)
- fever (in most but not all).

Assessment
The chest is often clear on auscultation – especially in early stages. Fine crackles may be heard. Chest X-rays may reveal little and can lead to delay. The GP may be thinking of asthma, an atypical chest infection or anxiety. If PCP is a possibility, look for evidence of HIV: see the guidance on assessment above and also boxed information on page 38.

Management/referral
Refer the patient urgently if you are concerned they may have PCP, which can only be diagnosed by hospital-based tests such as induced sputum and bronchoscopy. An HIV test may cause inappropriate delay.

This condition is also important to detect in any patient known to have HIV, even if they are on medication to prevent this. PCP is most often seen in those with CD4 counts of less than 200 cells/µl, but about 10 per cent have a CD4 above 200 cells/µl, so a CD4 at this level should not be a reason to exclude PCP.

TB and atypical mycobacterial disease

TB is an important and common presenting problem in HIV-infected patients in the UK. It can occur at CD4 counts above 200. People with HIV are more likely to develop symptoms and/or systemic infection with TB than those without HIV.

Atypical mycobacterial disease (*Mycobacterium avium intracellulare*) is a less common complication, associated with late-stage HIV infection.

See case study page 39

Symptoms

The patient may have a cough, fever, sweats, shortness of breath, weight loss or haemoptysis. They may have associated large, asymmetrical nodes.

Mycobacterium avium intracellulare may present with systemic symptoms and chest symptoms may or may not be present. Abnormal liver function tests and anaemia may be found.

> Guidelines recommend Anyone diagnosed with TB should be tested for HIV.

Assessment

As for TB in the HIV-negative (eg CXR), but look for evidence of HIV: see guidance on assessment on page 29 and also boxed information on page 38. *Mycobacterium avium intracellulare* is very unlikely in a patient without several clinical pointers to HIV disease because it occurs at very low CD4 counts.

Management/referral

Urgent outpatient or inpatient referral will be required, although an HIV test could also be arranged and may save time if the patient is not too unwell.

For guidance on assessment see box on page 29

Community-acquired chest infections

Chest infections which respond to the antibiotics usually employed in community settings are commoner in immunosuppressed patients.

> Guidelines recommend Anyone with bacterial pneumonia should be offered an HIV test.

Assessment

Look for evidence of HIV: see guidance on assessment on page 29, and also boxed information on page 38.

Management/referral

As usual for chest infections, but offer an HIV test if appropriate.

2. Conditions causing neurological and visual symptoms

> Guidelines recommend Anyone with cryptococcal or aseptic meningitis, space occupying lesion or peripheral neuropathy should be offered an HIV test.

A great variety of intracranial or peripheral neurological problems may occur in relation to HIV infection. Symptoms and signs include:

- headache, neck stiffness or photophobia
- focal neurological signs suggesting intracranial space occupying lesion (for example, lymphoma)
- peripheral neuropathy (especially sensory change or loss)
- confusion, memory loss, or disinhibition
- fits.

Cryptococcal meningitis
This may present with headaches without the classical symptoms or signs of meningism.

Assessment
Apart from a neurological assessment and general examination, look for evidence of HIV. See guidance on assessment on page 29.

Management/referral
The patient will need to be referred urgently. An HIV test may cause inappropriate delay if the patient is very unwell.

Toxoplasmosis
This may present with headaches, fever and focal neurological signs which may be progressive.

Assessment
Apart from a neurological assessment and general examination, look for evidence of HIV. See guidance on assessment on page 29.

Management/referral
The patient will need to be referred urgently. Waiting for an HIV test may cause inappropriate delay if the diagnosis is suspected.

Cerebral lymphoma
This may present with headaches, fever and focal neurological signs which may be progressive.

Assessment
Apart from a neurological assessment and general examination, look for evidence of HIV. See guidance on assessment on page 29.

Management/referral
The patient will need to be referred urgently. Waiting for an HIV test may cause inappropriate delay if the diagnosis is suspected.

Cytomegalovirus (CMV) infection of the retina
CMV infection of the retina causes blindness and can be treated, but earlier diagnosis improves the prognosis. It is mostly found in those who have CD4 counts of less than 100 cells/µl.

Guidelines recommend Anyone with suspected CMV or with any unexplained retinopathy should be offered an HIV test.

The patient may have:
- floaters
- reduced vision
- scotomas.

For CD4 counts see page 17

Assessment
Changes may be visible on fundoscopy, but the absence of changes should not alter management. Look for evidence of HIV: see guidance on assessment on page 29. CMV retinitis is very unlikely in a patient without several clinical pointers to HIV disease, because it occurs at very low CD4 counts.

For guidance on assessment see box on page 29

Management/referral
The patient will need to be referred urgently to ophthalmology. Waiting for the result of an HIV test may cause inappropriate delay if the patient is very unwell.

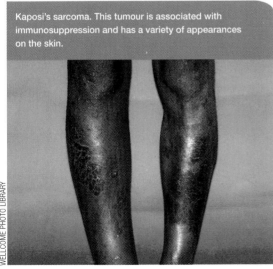

Kaposi's sarcoma. This tumour is associated with immunosuppression and has a variety of appearances on the skin.

WELLCOME PHOTO LIBRARY

3. Tumours associated with HIV

> Guidelines recommend Anyone diagnosed with lymphoma should routinely be offered an HIV test.

Lymphoma
Lymphoma may cause lymphadenopathy, fevers, night sweats and abdominal masses. It may be cerebral (see neurological problems, page 32).

Assessment
Look for evidence of HIV. See guidance on assessment on page 29.

Management/referral
As for any suspected cancer.

Cervical carcinoma
Cervical cancer may cause vaginal bleeding or discharge. Cytological abnormalities may also be a marker for underlying HIV infection.

Assessment and management/referral
As normal for suspected cervical cancer. Offer an HIV test if appropriate.

Kaposi's sarcoma (KS)

These tumours may occur in a variety of places. They most commonly appear as dark purple or brown intradermal lumps that sometimes look like bruises (but feel harder). KS may also be found in the mouth. Infiltration of the lungs or gut is rare but can be very serious, the latter causing GI bleeding.

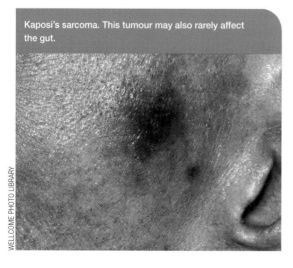

Kaposi's sarcoma. This tumour may also rarely affect the gut.

Assessment and management/referral
Refer to HIV specialist, may require urgent medical admission if lung or gut involvement.

WELLCOME PHOTO LIBRARY

4. Constitutional symptoms associated with HIV

Guidelines recommend Anyone with mononucleosis-like syndrome, PUO, weight loss of >10kg or lymphadenopathy of unknown cause should be offered an HIV test.

Constitutional symptoms may be caused by HIV itself, or by a related opportunistic infection (such as TB) or tumour (such as a lymphoma). Symptoms include:

- fever
- weight loss
- sweats
- lymphadenopathy (HIV is particularly likely if this persists in excess of three months, in two or more extra-inguinal sites and in the absence of any other cause).

See case study page 40

Assessment
Look for evidence of HIV.

For guidance on assessment see box on page 29

Management/referral
Urgent assessment is sometimes appropriate. For outpatient referrals arrange an HIV test beforehand to ensure that the appropriate clinic is identified and inform them of the result. For inpatient referrals, highlight the need for HIV testing in the referral letter.

5. Skin conditions

See case study page 41

Look out for common skin conditions that are particularly severe or hard to treat. Review the records for other evidence of HIV infection.

Examples include:

- **fungal infections**, such as tinea cruris, tinea pedis, pityriasis versicolor
- **viral infections**, such as shingles (especially if more than one dermatome is affected), *Molluscum contagiosum*, warts and herpes simplex
- **bacterial infections**, such as impetigo, folliculitis
- **Kaposi's sarcoma** (see above for description)
- **other skin conditions**, such as seborrhoeic dermatitis and psoriasis

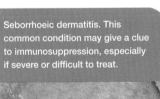

Seborrhoeic dermatitis. This common condition may give a clue to immunosuppression, especially if severe or difficult to treat.

Assessment
Look for evidence of HIV. See guidance on assessment on page 29, and also boxed information on page 38.

Management/referral
As usual, and arrange an HIV test if appropriate.

6. Conditions affecting the mouth

> Guidelines recommend Anyone with oral candidiasis and/or oral hairy leukoplakia should be offered an HIV test.

Immunosuppression can lead to a number of conditions affecting the mouth and examination of the mouth is key in assessment as some of the conditions may be asymptomatic. Examples include:

- **oral candidiasis** (thrush): not just a coated tongue, but thick white plaques on the buccal mucosa that could be scraped off with a tongue depressor. Oral candida can also have a red, fleshy appearance with fewer – or no – plaques and in this case can be harder to diagnose. Swabs are of little diagnostic value because of high carriage rates. Florid oral thrush should always lead to a consideration of whether the patient could be immunosuppressed
- **aphthous ulceration**
- **oral hairy leukoplakia**: causing whitish corrugations, typically on the side of the tongue. They cannot be scraped off. It is usually asymptomatic, but is pathognomic of immunosuppression. It is useful to look for this if you suspect a patient may have HIV disease (see photo on page 37)
- **Kaposi's sarcoma**: purple tumour, characteristically on the palate
- **gingivitis**
- **dental abscesses**.

Assessment
Look for evidence of HIV: see guidance on assessment on page 29, and also boxed information on page 38.

Management/referral
As usual and arrange an HIV test if appropriate.

7. Conditions affecting the upper and lower GI tract

> Guidelines recommend Anyone with chronic diarrhoea or oral/oesophageal candidiasis should be offered an HIV test.

Significant conditions include:
- **oesophageal candidiasis**: the patient presents with dysphagia suggestive of an oesophageal problem, but is highly likely to have concurrent oral thrush
- **diarrhoea** – persistent mild, or severe acute. There may be virtually any – or commonly no – causative organism found.

Assessment
Look for evidence of HIV.

Management/referral
As usual and arrange an HIV test if appropriate.

For guidance on assessment see box on page 29

Left to right:
1. Oral candida. This condition is an important indicator of immunosuppression.
2. Oral hairy leukoplakia. Pathognomic of immunosuppression.
3. Palatal Kaposi's sarcoma. This tumour gives another reason for careful examination of the mouth when looking for evidence of HIV.

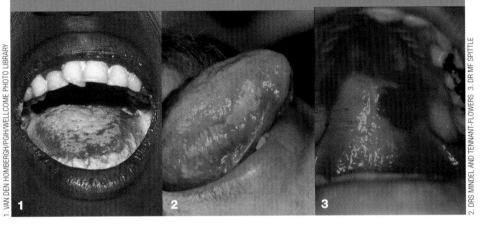

1. VAN DEN HOMBERGH/PGIH/WELLCOME PHOTO LIBRARY

2. DRS MINDEL AND TENNANT-FLOWERS 3. DR MF SPITTLE

8. Genital problems

> Guidelines recommend Anyone diagnosed with an STI should be routinely tested for HIV.

Sexually transmitted infections (STIs) such as genital herpes or genital warts may be more severe in the immunosuppressed patient. In addition, severe or difficult to treat genital candida may itself be a clue to immunosuppression. The diagnosis of any STI should lead to a consideration of the possibility of other STIs, including HIV.

See case study page 42

Assessment
Look for evidence of HIV: see guidance on assessment on page 29, and also boxed information on page 38.

Management/referral
As usual and arrange an HIV test if appropriate.

See also cervical cancer page 34

9. Haematological problems

Changes found on routine full blood counts may give a clue to immunosuppression. They may be severe enough to require urgent action, but are often more subtle, with few symptoms. Examples include anaemia, neutropenia, lymphopenia, thrombocytopenia and diffuse hypergammaglobulinemia.

> Guidelines recommend Offering an HIV test to anyone with:
> - neutropenia
> - anaemia
> - thrombocytopenia
> - any other unexplained blood dyscrasia.

Assessment
Look for evidence of HIV: see guidance on assessment on page 29, and also boxed information below.

Management/referral
As usual and arrange an HIV test if appropriate.

What to do if you suspect HIV infection may underlie the presenting problem

If the problem is clinically minor (seborrhoeic dermatitis in a patient who had multidermatomal shingles two months ago), it may be reasonable to arrange an early review of the patient in order to give yourself time to collect your thoughts. But don't risk losing patients to follow-up. Remember that resolution of the presenting problem does not mean that HIV has been ruled out.

- **Enquire** about weight loss, sweats, diarrhoea.
- **Examine** the patient for other signs of immunosuppression (mouth, skin and nodes, see pages 35-37).
- **Review** the records for evidence of HIV-associated problems in the last three years (see list, pages 30-38).
- **Discuss** the possibility of HIV with the patient to consider their risk.

For many GPs raising the subject of HIV with the patient is difficult. For more details on risk assessment, see page 45 and for suggested phrases for raising the question of an HIV test, see pages 47-49.

- **Decide on priorities**: is urgent assessment by a specialist required or can an HIV test be offered?

If the clinical picture is strongly suggestive of HIV, an apparent absence of risk of infection should not deter you from offering a test.

For more on risk assessment see page 45

case study

Late diagnosis of HIV and tuberculosis

Jemi is a 26-year-old woman who came to the UK from Sierra Leone two years ago. She saw her GP with a six-week history of fevers, intermittent cough and cervical lymphadenopathy. Nine months previously she had attended her GP with fatigue and was found to have mild anaemia. Now she was prescribed Penicillin V, which alleviated her symptoms for a few days. A week later she presented again with rigors, night sweats and weight loss. She was admitted to hospital for investigation of pyrexia of unknown origin with malaria at the top of the differential diagnosis.

She was found to have non-tender 'rubbery' lymphadenopathy in her axilliary, inguinal, supraclavicular and cervical areas. On admission she also had a fever of 39.4°C and a tachycardia. She was hypotensive, had 2-3cms hepatomegaly and otherwise no focal signs in her chest, abdomen or CNS.

She was treated with multiple antibiotics but did not improve. Following discussion with a member of the HIV team she reluctantly agreed to an HIV test, which was positive. She was eventually diagnosed with tuberculosis following sputum culture.

The history that emerged when she felt better was that she had been feeling 'ill' for at least six to eight weeks, and had had intermittent fevers (and some night sweats) for three months. She had been complaining of non-specific fatigue/malaise for at least eight or nine months, for which the full blood count had been the only investigation. She might not have agreed to an HIV test at that time, but an earlier diagnosis might have enabled her to avoid hospitalisation.

> She had been complaining of non-specific fatigue/malaise for at least eight or nine months, for which the full blood count had been the only investigation. She might not have agreed to an HIV test at that time, but an earlier diagnosis might have enabled her to avoid hospitalisation.

Learning points

- The *UK National Guidelines for HIV Testing 2008* recommend HIV testing for patients presenting with pyrexia of unknown origin and weight loss.
- HIV should be considered in people from areas of high HIV prevalence, regardless of their presentation.

case study

A delayed diagnosis

Ganesh is a 49-year-old divorced university lecturer. He attended his GP some months ago with diarrhoea and weight loss. Stool culture/microscopy revealed no apparent pathogen and there was little response to anti-diarrhoeal medication. He was referred to the local hospital where he was seen and placed on the waiting list for both upper GI endoscopy and a flexible sigmoidoscopy. This was performed four months after the original referral letter, his symptoms having continued and his overall weight loss being some 10 per cent of his original weight.

After the procedure he had to stay in hospital for two nights as he appeared to have developed an aspiration pneumonia. Broad-spectrum antibiotic treatment did very little and he was re-admitted four days later. Bronchoscopy confirmed a diagnosis of PCP, for which he was admitted and treated

without further complication.

The only recorded social history was that he was divorced and smoked 20 cigarettes daily. He was not embarrassed to tell the doctors that he had sex with other men, but nobody had ever asked him. He was not surprised by the subsequent HIV diagnosis. His CD4 count was 49 cells/μl and he has done well since starting combination antiretroviral therapy.

Learning points
- The *UK National Guidelines for HIV Testing 2008* recommend testing for patients presenting with persistent unresolved diarrhoea and weight loss.
- If the symptoms could indicate HIV infection it is important to offer an HIV test even if a risk assessment has not been done, or no risk behaviour has been disclosed by the patient.

case study

A 'low-risk' man

Russell is a 33-year-old of UK origin who first presented to the practice nurse during a new patient medical following a house move. He lived with his girlfriend of eight years. At registration he complained of a rash on his face. This was red, dry and flaky and affected his forehead and his naso-labial folds. He was given a topical hydrocortisone/antifungal cream.

Twelve months later he returned to the practice and saw a locum GP following three days of non-specific abdominal pain and fever. He returned again to the practice after 10 days with a dry cough, fatigue and lethargy. He was given a broad-spectrum antibiotic but 14 days later was worse, and had developed a generalised maculopapular rash. The facial rash had returned, since he had run out of cream. He had lost 4kg of weight.

Frustrated at being off work for so long, he requested a referral to the local hospital where he was seen by a consultant physician three weeks later. Tests carried out by the GP in advance revealed a slight thrombocytopenia, mild elevation of his liver transaminases and a raised ESR. A chest X-ray was reported as normal. Russell was asked if he had ever injected drugs and stated that he had not done so. Serology for hepatitis B was negative. Physical examination by the hospital consultant revealed no abnormalities and an ultrasound of his liver was arranged.

Another three weeks passed, with no scan appointment arriving. Russell reported a worsening of his cough and extreme fatigue. He had marked dyspnoea on exertion. Two days later his girlfriend took him to casualty. By this time his dyspnoea had worsened, his weight loss continued and he had a dry cough. He was found to be tachypnoeic and hypoxic. His CXR showed patchy shadowing. The medical team felt he probably had *Pneumocystis* pneumonia (PCP). This was later confirmed on bronchoscopy. Russell tested positive for HIV and his CD4 count was only 10 cells/µl. Following the successful treatment of his PCP and initiation of antiretroviral therapy, he returned to work and remains well.

With no apparent risk factors to suggest a significant probability of HIV infection, and with such an insidious onset, the diagnosis eluded many practitioners until Russell was quite seriously ill. It is probable that he acquired HIV through a sexual contact many years previously when he was travelling in Thailand and South East Asia in his student years.

> With no apparent risk factors to suggest a significant probability of HIV infection, and with such an insidious onset, the diagnosis eluded many practitioners until Russell was quite seriously ill.

Learning points
- Some people with HIV have no obvious risk factors for HIV infection.
- HIV infection can often exacerbate common skin conditions.
- Consider PCP in patients with recent onset dyspnoea or where atypical or severe respiratory infection is possible.
- Don't forget to ask about travel to areas of high HIV prevalence when taking a history.

case study

A newly registered African woman

Haruzivi is a 34-year-old Zimbabwean carer who had just registered with her GP. Her new patient check noted that her child had died in Zimbabwe before she came to this country three years ago. When her records came they showed she had had a previous abnormal smear (CIN 1).

Haruzivi attended the surgery because of recurrent genital itching. She described her current health as good. On examination she was found to have genital herpes and *Molluscum contagiosum*. The GP also found cervical lymphadenopathy. She had no other rashes and no oral conditions suggestive of HIV. On further questioning her GP ascertained she had no history of previous sexually transmitted infections and had never been tested for HIV. The GP suggested that an HIV test was done, and the patient agreed. The result was positive, information which Haruzivi took surprisingly well.

Haruzivi was referred to the HIV clinic and soon after commenced on ART. Currently, she is quite well and continues to work. On several occasions since her diagnosis she has thanked her GP for suggesting the HIV test. She had felt she was not at risk and is glad that she had the test before she became seriously unwell.

Learning points

- HIV should be considered in people from areas of high HIV prevalence, regardless of their presentation.
- The presence of conditions that may be HIV-related can be used to initiate discussions about HIV testing.

HIV testing in primary care

Reducing the amount of undiagnosed HIV in the UK is a priority. Individuals who know they are infected with HIV have significant advantages over those who are infected but unaware of this. They will:

- benefit from current treatments resulting in an improved prognosis
- have information which may enable them to avoid passing on the virus
- become less infectious once on ART
- have the opportunity to reflect and plan ahead.

> See the *UK National Guidelines for HIV Testing 2008* at www.bhiva.org, www.bashh.org and www.britishinfection.org

1. The practicalities

What is the HIV test?

> See page 26 for information on primary HIV infection

There are different types of HIV test. The most commonly used modern tests detect both HIV antibodies and antigens. It is important to remember that occasionally the test may not become positive until one month or more after the person has become infected (the window period) and current guidance recommends a repeat test at three months after the most recent risk.

In primary HIV infection, an HIV test will usually be positive but may be negative or equivocal.

> For the types of HIV test including POCT see pages 15-16

Rapid point-of-care tests (POCTs) are useful in many situations where an instant result is needed and you may decide that they are appropriate for use in your practice if you and your staff feel confident to deal with a reactive result and can incorporate their use into your normal working routines. However, POCTs can have some disadvantages. GPs will often want to take a full blood sample anyway for other reasons such as sickle cell screening, lipids or viral hepatitis. Also, the very short interval between testing and result may not be ideal if you prefer to have time to think and plan before giving a positive result. If considering POCTs, you should seek expert advice on their selection and use.

USEFUL INFO

Recent joint guidelines provide more detailed advice for doctors (Association of British Insurers & British Medical Association (2010) *Medical information and insurance: joint guidelines from the British Medical Association and the Association of British Insurers*). Insurers should only ask whether the applicant has tested positive for HIV. For updated guidance on confidentiality from the GMC, see *Confidentiality* (2009) at www.gmc-uk.org – GPs should be guided by clinical need above all other considerations.

HIV testing and insurance reports

GPs should not allow insurance concerns to compromise patient care: if an HIV test is appropriate, it should be offered. In the past there has been a reluctance to use HIV tests as a diagnostic tool in primary care.

This has been partly due to concerns that a patient or doctor may have to declare an HIV test (regardless of the result) on an insurance application or medical report form. However, as long ago as 1994, the Association of British Insurers stated that a negative HIV test should not affect the application.

Laboratory support

The lab will need a clotted sample. Some smaller hospital laboratories only run HIV tests on certain days. Larger hospitals have several runs on a daily basis and have access to POCTs. Phone the lab to check:

- when HIV tests are processed
- when the results will be available
- what their procedure will be if they find an apparent positive.

    Typically a lab will call when they find a positive result, and request a repeat sample.

Links with specialist HIV treatment centre(s)

The best time to find out about local HIV treatment centres and to establish links with them is before you have a patient who tests positive. This will ensure that clear referral pathways are in place, including details of who to contact if a patient needs to be seen urgently by a specialist.

Computer and paper systems to support HIV testing

See page 85 for discussion of systems and record keeping.

2. When should an HIV test be offered?

There are a number of circumstances in which it is appropriate to conduct an HIV test in primary care:

- patient request
- opportunistic testing – when an HIV test is offered to someone who might be at risk
- diagnostic testing – when an HIV test is done because someone has an indicator condition, or symptoms or signs of HIV infection
- screening – for example antenatal screening, or routine offering of the test to someone who has had a diagnosis of an STI.

    If the test is offered on a routine or opt-out basis, evidence suggests it makes offering the test easier as it is perceived as non-judgemental and it is more likely to be accepted.

The patient who requests an HIV test

Patients requesting an HIV test will have a reason. You may choose to be reassuring but avoid discouraging patients from testing and take care before declining to test.

For the window period and different types of HIV test see pages 15-16

Be flexible: some people with HIV may have no apparent risk. Patients may or may not be prepared to discuss their risks with you. You do not always need to know what risk there was, as long as the patient understands the significance of the window period and what constitutes risk. If doubts remain, arrange a second test at the appropriate time.

The patient may have an identified risk

As HIV infection may be asymptomatic for some time, the only hope of improving primary care detection rates in this group is if clinicians are willing and able to discuss risk of HIV and offer tests as appropriate. Risk of HIV can be identified through drug and sexual history taking for the purposes of health promotion.

The following should be offered a test if they have never been tested, or if they have been at risk since their last test. Those who:

- have a current or former sexual partner who is infected with HIV, or from an area with a high prevalence of HIV or who was an injecting drug user
- are men who have had sex with another man
- are female sexual contacts of men who have sex with men
- are from an area with a high prevalence of HIV (although risk should be discussed without pre-judgement as many people in this group may be at no risk)
- have had multiple sexual partners
- have a history of sexually transmitted infection
- have a history of injecting drug use
- have been raped (although in an acute situation this is best managed by specialist services if the patient will attend)
- have had blood transfusions, transplants or other risk prone procedures in countries without rigorous procedures for HIV screening
- may have had an occupational exposure.

Careful condom use will have offered significant protection – this should be acknowledged, even if testing still goes ahead. Be ready to test anyone who requests an HIV test after their history has been taken, even if they have not indicated a specific risk to you.

> **IMPORTANT!**
> Make sure all pregnant women are offered and recommended an HIV test. Interventions can reduce the risk of mother-to-child transmission from over 20 per cent to less than 1 per cent.

For clinical diagnosis see box on page 29

For preventing mother-to-child transmission see page 20

See *Time to test for HIV: expanded healthcare and community HIV testing in England* at www.hpa.org.uk

The patient may have symptoms or signs suggestive of HIV disease

See pages 27-36 for clinical diagnosis and pages 47-49 for communication strategies in this context.

The patient may be in a group offered screening tests for HIV

Screening will sometimes be offered in a specialist setting, and sometimes in primary care. For example:

- **women in antenatal care**, in order to prevent mother-to-child transmission
- **those found to have conditions which may be associated with HIV** (such as TB, lymphoma, hepatitis B or C, syphilis or other STIs). It is important that the value of the HIV test is explained to the patient.

Areas in the UK with high local diagnosed HIV prevalence (greater than two in 1,000)

Based on cost-effectiveness data from the US, the *UK National Guidelines for HIV Testing 2008* recommend that HIV testing should be considered for all new patient registrations in primary care and routine medical admissions in areas of local diagnosed HIV prevalence equal to or greater than two in 1,000. The results of UK pilot studies of this approach have now been published by the Health Protection Agency and the data support the recommendation. However, its wide-scale implementation will depend on local commissioning priorities and appropriate resourcing, training and support for practices.

Opportunities to raise the subject of an HIV test may arise:

- before a sexual history has been taken – perhaps in a contraception or cervical screening consultation
- once a sexual history has been taken – perhaps the patient has identified risk factors for HIV
- when a history of injecting drug use has been identified
- in a new patient check during a discussion about sexual health
- if your practice is in an area of high local HIV prevalence.

Remember to emphasise the benefits of earlier HIV diagnosis.

Useful phrases to help bring up HIV testing

(With thanks to Sexual Health in Practice (SHIP), www.ship.bham.nhs.uk)

If the patient has signs and symptoms of infection ▶

Illnesses like this are usually caused by viruses, for example the glandular fever or flu virus. Some quite rare viruses can also be a cause, and it is important that I don't miss them if they occur. I don't know if you are at risk, but HIV is one of these.

The problems that you have had recently are quite common, and usually minor. However, very occasionally they can give a clue that your immune system is not working as well as it should.

I don't know if you are at risk of HIV, but this is one condition that can affect the immune system. Could I ask you some questions to see if you could be at risk?

From what you tell me you are quite unlikely to have HIV but I think it would be wise to do a test anyway so that we can be sure. Is that OK?

If the patient is in a group offered screening, or a group at higher risk of HIV infection ▶

All pregnant women are automatically offered a test for syphilis, hepatitis B, HIV and rubella – however we think it's better to have this information before you get pregnant. Would you like a test?

Current advice is that everyone who has injected drugs in the past should be offered a test for HIV, because this condition responds so well to treatment. Have you ever considered having a test?

[To a patient with an STI, eg herpes or warts] I would always recommend chlamydia and HIV tests, as you may have been at risk of these infections too – and they are treatable.

If the patient is in a group offered screening, or a group at higher risk of HIV infection (cont'd) ▶

[To a male patient] Because two of your partners in the last year have been male, it is possible that you are at higher risk of HIV. Have you ever considered having an HIV test?

We find that quite a lot of young men are at risk of having sexual health problems. Could I ask you a few questions to see if you are at risk?

OK, so you'd like a test for chlamydia. Would you like an HIV test too?

So you had a negative test for HIV a year ago – is there any reason you wouldn't want another check now?

There is a lot of HIV in your home country, I think. Do you know anyone who is affected? Have you ever had a test?

As part of general holistic care and 'good doctoring' ▶

We are trying to do a lot more HIV testing because undiagnosed HIV can do a lot of damage and we know the infection responds so well to treatment.

There is really quite a lot of undiagnosed HIV in this area so we are trying to increase our testing rates as people do much better if they know they have it.

We include an HIV test in our new patient check for everyone because we're in a part of the country where there are higher than average levels of HIV and we wouldn't want to miss anyone. Is that OK?

As part of general holistic care (cont'd) ▼

> But doctor – do you really think I need to have an HIV test?

> Well I don't think it's my job to dissuade anyone from having an HIV test at present. Currently doctors are doing too few tests, not too many. I would say: if in doubt, test.

3. The pre-test discussion

The *UK National Guidelines for HIV Testing 2008* state that the primary purpose of pre-test discussion is to establish informed consent to the HIV test and that lengthy pre-test counselling is not required unless a patient requests or needs it. The time a discussion takes is extremely variable, but in a well-informed, reasonably low risk person it may take just a few minutes.

Essential elements of the pre-test discussion
The benefits of HIV testing
If the patient gets a negative HIV test result:
- they have the reassurance that they do not have HIV
- they can continue to take steps to avoid HIV
- their current condition can be treated without being affected by HIV.

If the patient gets a positive HIV test result:

IMPORTANT!
The essential aspects that need to be covered in the pre-test discussion are:
- the benefits of testing for the individual
- details of how the result will be given.

- there are effective treatments that will stop them getting ill with HIV-related diseases
- they can take steps to avoid passing it on to their sexual partners
- treatment for any other conditions can be adjusted, if necessary, to make sure that treatment is most effective
- people with HIV can have healthy children if they know their HIV status early on in pregnancy
- they will have more control over who to tell, and when, than if they found out while very ill with HIV infection.

Check whether you have their contact details

Record contact details, and check their preferred method of contact and any possible problems with leaving messages or talking. You will be glad of this if the patient fails to attend for a result that turned out to be positive.

See BASHH/
MedFASH (2010)
*Standards for the
management of
sexually transmitted
infections (STIs)* at
www.bashh.org and
www.medfash.org.uk

Arrange an appointment for the result to be given

Try to ensure that you are not going to give a result at a bad time – for example, a Friday evening surgery. A good rule is to arrange to give the result face to face. If the result is negative, you can always ring them instead if that is more convenient and saves them a repeat visit. Nurses may also give negative HIV results on the phone. If you arrange to give the result by phone, and then later ask them to come to the surgery instead because the result is positive, this can create unnecessary anxiety.

A 'no news is good news' policy is not considered good practice for HIV and STI test results, according to the British Association for Sexual Health and HIV.

Check whether the patient has given clear consent to HIV (or other) tests

Informed consent must be obtained before any test. Ask them directly if they agree to the HIV test. Written consent is not required.

See HIV testing
aide-memoire on
page 90

Other areas sometimes covered in a pre-test discussion

Given here is a breakdown of further issues that might be covered in a pre-test discussion with a patient who needs or requests it. Not all areas will need to be covered with all patients. A checklist is given on page 90 which can be used as an aide-memoire by the GP or practice nurse.

i) Check the patient's understanding of HIV

Assess their understanding of different transmission routes and of the difference between HIV and AIDS. Some patients believe that if they have had any blood tests in the past, they will automatically have been tested for HIV. Also, the patient should understand the significance of the window period and that a repeat test may be needed.

ii) Discuss risk to date

Knowing the nature of the risk enables you to tailor advice on risk reduction, and knowing the timing of risk(s) is important because of the window period (see pages 15-16). If doubt about the window period remains, simply arrange a second test in three months.

If the patient does not wish to discuss their risk, but wishes to go ahead with a test, they should be able to do so as long as the benefits of discussing risk have been mentioned.

See page 45 for risks that may be discussed. If the patient is unwilling to go into detail, it may be best simply to address the issues on the HIV aide-memoire (page 90) in order to maintain the doctor-patient relationship.

iii) Discuss future risk and risk reduction

This may be the first opportunity that a patient has had to discuss risk reduction. It is best to discuss safer sexual practices and safer injecting practices before the test, not least because risks may be taken before the patient is next seen. If a repeat test is to be arranged, emphasise that if HIV is transmitted between now and the next test, it may not show up in that result. Also, if the patient has recently been exposed, and therefore possibly recently infected, they may well be highly infectious so they should be encouraged to consider this and practice risk reduction before the repeat test.

See more on the timing of risks on page 16

iv) Discuss the implications of a positive test

How is the patient likely to react if the result is positive? What would their main concerns be if they tested positive? Who would they tell? Who would they not tell? What will be the reactions be of those they might tell? What might be the implications for their partner? For their work?

Bear in mind that a small minority of patients may tell you that a positive HIV test result would be too much to bear and they might self-harm in some way. It is important to use your judgement about whether a test in general practice under these circumstances is appropriate, or if the patient may benefit from the additional support that a test in GUM could offer.

v) Explain confidentiality

Explain that a positive test result will need to be recorded in their medical records so that their healthcare remains safe and appropriate. Reassure the patient that such records are stored securely and are only available to the relevant healthcare professionals.

If the patient has concerns about how HIV testing might affect insurance applications:

- explain that a positive result would have to be disclosed to insurance companies if requested
- emphasise that negative tests do not have to be disclosed.

vi) Discuss how they will cope with the wait

Ask the patient to consider who knows they are having a test, and who it is safe to tell. Advise the patient not to drink alcohol or take recreational drugs on the day of the result. Consider whether there is any written information that should be given to the patient.

vii) Consider if the test is best conducted in primary care

In people with psychological or emotional problems, or those with additional counselling needs, a referral to GUM services for testing may be appropriate. This should be balanced against the benefits of having a test conducted in familiar surroundings and by a clinician known to the patient.

viii) Consider whether other tests are appropriate

It may be appropriate to request other tests at the same time as HIV. For example:

- if the risk is considered to be due to needle sharing, talk to the patient about testing for hepatitis B and C
- if the risk is unprotected sexual intercourse – particularly if the risk appears high – then you may wish to discuss tests for other STIs such as chlamydia or hepatitis B.

    There is a growing trend for specialist clinics to offer routine tests for hepatitis B and C alongside HIV. Consider the need for immunisation against hepatitis B.

ix) Consider whether repeat tests are required

For more detail on the window period see pages 15-16

Ensure the patient understands if they are going to need a repeat test (to cover the window period) before HIV infection can be ruled out.

x) Check if the patient has a supply of appropriate condoms and lubricant

Some practices can provide condoms and lubricant, but if not, signposting to GUM, contraceptive services or gay men's health organisations where free condoms and lubricant are available is helpful.

4. Giving the result

- **If the result is negative**, you need to consider whether the patient needs a further test because of the window period.
- **If the result is positive**, there are many things you need to consider before the patient attends.

Preparing to give a positive result

You will have time to collect your thoughts and seek advice, because the lab is likely to phone the result through and ask for a repeat sample.

IMPORTANT!
When giving a negative result, don't forget to reinforce advice about minimising risk, if appropriate.

Remember:

- you already have skills in discussing very difficult things
- the patient chose you to do their test, so they chose you to give them the result.

Review the notes from the consultation when you took the test. If the pre-test discussion was brief, there may not be very much information, so prepare to ask the patient to consider the following:
- what is their main concern should the test be positive?
- who knows they were being tested?
- where do they get support?
- is there a partner whose needs you should discuss with the patient? (Formal partner notification should be addressed by the HIV clinic.)

Consider referral arrangements:

See 'the newly diagnosed patient' on page 58

- the patient will need to be referred to a specialist HIV clinic for assessment within two weeks of testing positive so an appointment can be made in advance. Patients may have their own preferences for treatment centres so should be involved in this decision wherever possible
- have phone numbers of support organisations and relevant literature available.

When the patient attends
Give the result soon after the patient is in the room and has sat down. Delaying disclosure can heighten anxiety. This allows you more time to attend to and deal with the patient's reactions. Some patients are expecting a positive result and may be quite calm. Indeed, some may have already come to terms with being positive. A calm exterior can also mask a sense of shock.

In the case of a positive result, listen carefully and make the discussion focused and tailored to the individual.

You should emphasise the positive aspects: patients are better off knowing that they have HIV.

When the consultation is coming to an end:
- give the patient the details of any appointment that you have arranged
- remember that risk reduction advice to protect partners will need to be addressed at some point, but this may be hard for the patient to take in at this consultation
- arrange to follow up the patient within a few days as they may well have additional questions and it will give you the opportunity to check that referral to the specialist service has been actioned.

case study

An opportunity to test for HIV

Pascal, aged 26, attended the practice nurse for a new patient check. He was an accountant, and generally fit and well with no significant past medical history. The practice encouraged sexual health promotion, and the nurse raised the subject after other aspects of the check were complete.

She asked him if it was okay if she asked questions to see if he could be at risk of any sexual health problems. He agreed, but seemed to become a bit guarded. The nurse took a partner history according to her routine, avoiding assumptions. The patient opened up and relaxed, and shortly explained that he wasn't living alone as he had told her, but was gay and living with his partner of three years. He felt this relationship was mutually monogamous, but he had had several partners prior to this. She asked about condom use and established that he had had significant risk of exposure to HIV through several 'casual' sexual contacts in years gone by. Pascal explained that he had always meant to have a test for HIV, but never got round to it. He had also discussed it with his partner in the past, but more recently the subject had been forgotten.

After discussion it was agreed that Pascal would suggest to his partner that he also registered 'as it seems a really nice practice'. The nurse agreed she would be happy to arrange an HIV test for both of them. In due course, both attended. The HIV tests were negative. They were very grateful to the nurse for having dealt with an issue that had been a suppressed but niggling worry.

> The HIV tests were negative. They were very grateful to the nurse for having dealt with an issue that had been a suppressed but niggling worry.

Learning points:
- Offering the HIV test can allay anxiety even where the result is negative.
- A negative result is a good opportunity for sexual health promotion.

Summary: how to improve HIV detection in your practice

Familiarise GPs and practice nurses in the team with:
- the more HIV-specific aspects of primary HIV infection, and be ready to ask about them in patients with a 'glandular fever-like' illness (pages 26-27)
- those urgent conditions that may present in patients whose HIV infection remains undiagnosed, most importantly PCP (pages 29-30)
- those indicator conditions that are associated with HIV infection (pages 29-38), especially if they have had:
  - more than one in the last two to three years; or
  - an unusually difficult to treat or severe form of these conditions
- risk factors for HIV which should prompt an offer of an HIV test (see page 45).

Print off the clinical indicator conditions table from the 2008 HIV testing guidelines (at the back of this booklet) and put it up in all consulting rooms.

Plan and practise strategies for discussing HIV with patients in different clinical circumstances.

Take steps to incorporate HIV testing into the health promotion work of the practice nurse team.

Consider including the HIV test in all new patient registrations if local diagnosed HIV prevalence is equal to or greater than two in 1,000.

Arrange a practice development session on HIV and STI testing – your local GUM service could help, or look at online learning options such as e-GP.

Section 3

Clinical care for people with HIV

IN THIS SECTION

Clinical care for people with HIV

HIV is increasingly managed as a chronic disease, with many individuals surviving for long periods. This, along with other changes in health policy, is shifting the emphasis of care towards partnership between specialist centres and primary care.

Patients with HIV

1. The newly diagnosed patient

Unfortunately, HIV infection is still a stigmatised condition and thus telling friends, family or colleagues is never easy. Some people will not be prepared to absorb fully the news of a positive test result. Even if they received in-depth pre-test discussion, some may need considerable support over time.

A significant number of women with HIV have been identified through antenatal screening. Such women may be facing a truly challenging range of issues: a newly diagnosed and serious medical condition, starting life-long medication, a pregnancy and whether to continue with it, the possibility that existing children and/or their partner are infected, all at the same time.

2. The patient who informs you they have HIV

A patient may inform their GP or practice nurse that they have HIV. Many patients with long-standing HIV infection can be considered 'expert patients' and some of these may be proactive in involving you in their general medical care.

Others may be more anxious about divulging this information. It may take some time before a patient with HIV chooses to disclose this to their GP, or they may find that illness forces the decision. They may require reassurance about the confidentiality of their records and the attitudes of practice staff who will need to know about their HIV status. Communication with the specialist clinic should be established as soon as possible.

Health promotion, screening and immunisation for people with HIV

1. Cardiovascular disease prevention
Research indicates that people with HIV are at higher risk from cardiovascular disease, although the mechanism of action is unclear. This appears to be particularly true for those who are not yet on antiretroviral therapy (ART). In addition, dyslipidemias and diabetes are associated with ART (see ART side effects, page 71). Effort should therefore be put into promoting healthy diets, exercise, alcohol control, blood pressure checks and smoking cessation. There are no recorded interactions between ART and varenicline. If in doubt, however, seek expert advice.

2. Cervical screening

See case study
page 60

Women with HIV are more at risk from HPV-related disease, including cervical cancer and warts. All women with HIV infection should have annual smears with more frequent follow-up and colposcopy if abnormalities are found.

3. Immunisation

See Department of Heath *Immunisation against infectious diseases* at www.dh.gov.uk

The practice can and should play a key role in immunising patients who have HIV. Current advice can be found in the *BHIVA Guidelines for the immunization of HIV-infected adults* (2008) which are very useful and practical for GPs. 'The Green Book' (Department of Health: Immunisation against infectious disease) is also very helpful. It can be viewed online where it is updated regularly.

Individuals with HIV infection should not normally receive BCG, cholera, or oral typhoid. Live oral polio (Sabin) immunisation should not be given due to the small risk of contact with excreted live vaccine. All inactivated immunisations such as pertussis, diphtheria, tetanus, *inactivated* polio (Salk), typhoid, and meningitis C are safe. Specialist advice from the HIV unit should be obtained where appropriate.

See BHIVA (2008) *Guidelines for the immunization of HIV-infected adults* at www.bhiva.org

Adults with HIV should be offered:
- influenza immunisation each year
- hepatitis B testing and immunisation as appropriate
- hepatitis A immunisation for men who have sex with men
- pneumococcal vaccination
- novel H1N1 (swine flu).

Specialist advice should be sought from the paediatric team about immunisation of children infected with HIV, and children of parents with HIV.

If a baby is born to a mother with HIV, transmitted infection will usually have been identified by eight weeks. Inactivated polio should be given if any family members are immunosuppressed, or if there is doubt about the baby's status.

4. Advice and immunisation for international travel

Hepatitis A and B vaccination should be offered as appropriate. It is important to remember to check hepatitis B titres. For those who do not respond to hepatitis B vaccination, specialist advice should be sought. The BHIVA guidelines provide more detailed information.

Malaria prophylaxis is used, but interactions with ART can occur. The antiretroviral, ritonavir, for example, can interact with several antimalarials. Check on www.hiv-druginteractions.org

For patients with HIV travelling to areas where medical support may be difficult to obtain, GPs might supply a couple of courses of ciprofloxacin for travellers' diarrhoea, together with advice on hygiene and food preparation.

Advice on safer sex and the avoidance of sexually transmitted infections may need to be reinforced.

> **USEFUL INFO**
> Some countries restrict entry for those with HIV. Patients should check with the relevant embassy or embassies before planning their trip. See www.aidsmap.com for a list of these countries.

case study

A case of missing smears?

Consuela is a 40-year-old woman from South America who registered with the practice in 2004. She had moved to the UK some 13 years previously and had been under the care of another practice in the locality, but switched when she changed address. Consuela was already aware of her positive HIV status when she registered, but did not disclose this to the practice. Over the next two years she did not attend the surgery very often and did not respond to invitations for cervical screening. The practice nurse had tried frequently to call her in. On the phone on one occasion Consuela told the practice nurse that a smear test had been done in a 'clinic appointment' at the hospital. The nurse asked her to bring a copy of the result but this was not forthcoming.

In 2007 Consuela became pregnant and was duly referred to the antenatal unit at the same hospital where she was accessing her HIV care. The pregnancy was uncomplicated and she delivered a girl by normal delivery. The baby has also since been registered with the practice and she has been fully

vaccinated; she is HIV-negative.

In 2009 an unexpected hospital smear result arrived at the practice showing severe squamous dyskaryosis present with features suspicious of invasion; colposcopy was recommended. There had been no symptoms. Within six weeks a radical hysterectomy had been performed with lymph node dissection, although there was evidence of micro-invasion confirmed on histology. Consuela is under the close supervision of the gynaecologist and the specialist oncology unit. This year Consuela has had her first post-operative vaginal vault smear which shows moderate squamous dyskaryosis and it is likely that she will need chemotherapy. This is being planned.

Learning points
- Women with HIV are at higher risk of cervical cancer and should have annual screening tests.
- Practices should liaise closely with HIV clinics to ensure the tests have been done and results are available.

Patients may also be offered a concise medical summary, including prescribed medication, in case of illness abroad. Some drugs, especially opiates, may need a licence from the Home Office. Also, check the entry requirements for the country concerned to ensure they do not deny entry to those with HIV. A list can be found on the aidsmap website (see useful sources for patients in Quick reference on page 104).

Sexual and reproductive health

1. Sexual health advice

Healthcare workers need to be able to discuss sexual practices with patients living with HIV. Many people find it difficult to maintain safer sex, so practitioners should be supportive and avoid criticism. Ideally, practices should provide condoms and (for anal sex) lubricant, but if not, signposting to services which provide free supplies is helpful.

Support from an expert counsellor or health adviser can be helpful in addressing difficulties related to HIV disclosure, or with adopting or maintaining safer sexual behaviour to prevent onward HIV transmission and protect against the risk of STIs. Expert advice may also be needed to address concerns about the (albeit unlikely) possibility of criminal prosecution if HIV transmission occurs.

It is helpful to make sure the patient with HIV is aware of the availability of post-exposure prophylaxis following sexual exposure (PEPSE) should an HIV-negative partner be exposed to HIV (see page 81).

Effective ART significantly reduces the risk of HIV transmission. Knowing this can reduce anxiety about the potential for accidental sexual transmission of HIV and may even be a factor in the decision to commence therapy. If the plasma viral load has been undetectable for more than six months, the risk of transmission is very low, although an undetermined residual risk of transmission is likely to exist. Condom use is recommended to reduce any residual risk; this is probably higher for anal than for vaginal or oral sex and increases with inadequate adherence to ART. The presence of STIs in either partner may have a dramatic effect on HIV transmission, so continued condom use is strongly recommended for those at continued risk, as are regular checks for other STIs.

Even in couples where both partners have HIV, condom use is recommended if either is non-monogamous because of the potential risk of acquiring other STIs. Some STIs are harder to treat in those with HIV, while hepatitis C has become epidemic among men with HIV who have sex with men, between whom it is mostly sexually transmitted. Regular sexual health checks are therefore important. Superinfection with a drug-resistant strain of HIV (thus limiting future treatment options) is also possible, although this has been observed far less frequently than initially anticipated.

For more, see BASHH/BHIVA/FSRH (2008) UK guidelines for the management of sexual and reproductive health of people living with HIV infection at www.bhiva.org

2. Contraception

Contraceptive choice for HIV-infected women may be limited by interactions with ART as the most commonly used ART combinations include enzyme inducing drugs (the PIs and NNRTIs). Condoms are a useful additional precaution against pregnancy where the efficacy of the primary contraceptive choice may be reduced and remain the only method proven to reduce the risk of HIV transmission.

See Faculty of Sexual and Reproductive Healthcare (2011) *Clinical Guidance: Drug Interactions with Hormonal Contraception* at www.fsrh.org

Oral contraceptives and patches

The combined oral contraceptive (COC), progestogen-only pill (POP) and hormonal patches may have reduced effectiveness with some antiretroviral combinations (including most first-line combinations) due to enzyme induction, and expert advice should be sought. Newer drugs such as maraviroc and etravirine do not interact with steroid hormones.

Long acting reversible contraception

The efficacy of the IUD, the IUS or depot medroxyprogesterone acetate injections (at the usual intervals) does not appear to be affected by enzyme inducing drugs. Implants, however, are potentially affected by interactions with enzyme inducing HIV medications – there have been cases of them failing in women on efavirenz – so switching to another method, or using condoms in addition, is recommended.

Emergency contraception

The copper IUD is the most effective method and will not be affected by drug interactions.

Doubling the dose of levonorgestrel (*Levonelle*) is generally advised for women on medication that interacts with progestogens (efavirenz, nevirapine, most protease inhibitors) although this is unlicensed. For women on other antiretrovirals this is not necessary; if in doubt a double dose may be appropriate as levonorgestrel side effects are few.

In the absence of data on its use by women taking enzyme inducing drugs, doubling the dose of ulipristal acetate (*ellaOne*) is not advised. Ulipristal acetate should not be used by women using enzyme inducing drugs or who have stopped them within the last four weeks.

See Faculty of Sexual and Reproductive Healthcare (2009) *UK Medical Eligibility Criteria for Contraceptive Use* at www.fsrh.org

The *UK Medical Eligibility Criteria for Contraceptive Use* provide detailed guidance on other factors which may influence contraceptive choice. Further information and up-to-date advice should always be sought from specialist services if there is uncertainty.

3. Fertility and assisted conception

Some couples with one partner infected with HIV will want to start a family. This is an area which will be managed by specialists, but it is useful to have some knowledge of the options to discuss with patients, should they raise the matter.

If the man has HIV infection, donor insemination is an option. For conception using the infected partner's sperm, the safest method is one called 'sperm washing'. This is very safe as long as the 'washed' sperm is retested for HIV, and no transmissions have been documented. Further information should be sought from the HIV specialist if a couple are interested. Sperm washing may be funded by the NHS but is decided on a case-by-case basis and access may differ across different parts of the UK.

If it is the woman who has HIV infection, she can establish when she is ovulating using ovulation kits, and then artificially inseminate using semen from her partner. Many successful pregnancies have resulted from this technique. This method is completely safe for the male partner.

Where the HIV-infected partner is on successful ART, a couple can also choose unprotected sexual intercourse which is timed to reduce the frequency of exposure (and thus the risk). If the man is on effective ART with an undetectable plasma viral load then the risk of transmission to a female partner is very low indeed. However, some men have detectable HIV in the semen even if it is undetectable in blood so the possibility of HIV infection cannot be entirely ruled out (see Sexual health advice above). It is important to counsel that very low risk does not mean zero risk. In the future pre-exposure prophylaxis (PrEP) – where the HIV-negative partner takes ART for a short time before and after the unprotected intercourse – may be offered. There are a few cases where it has been used, but it is unlicensed and not routinely recommended at present. Trials to establish its efficacy are ongoing.

Sub-fertility should be addressed in the usual way, although HIV status should be made clear if the couple are referred.

4. Antenatal and postnatal care

Many women with HIV are well and actively choose pregnancy. Some may have an unplanned pregnancy that they choose to continue. Some may have undergone the traumatic experience of discovering through antenatal HIV testing that they were infected with HIV.

Managing the pregnancy of a woman with HIV is strongly influenced by the need to prevent transmission to the baby. The risk of transmission can be reduced from around 20 per cent to under 1 per cent by the interventions given on page 20.

Support of bottle feeding

Although there is evidence that ART reduces HIV viral load in breast milk, the complete avoidance of breastfeeding for infants born to mothers with HIV is still recommended, regardless of maternal disease status, viral load or treatment. Support for bottle feeding should be offered and GPs may be able to prescribe infant formula milk if they feel it is appropriate.

This message may not be accepted by all mothers with HIV as, for some groups, breastfeeding has deep symbolic meaning. Avoidance of breastfeeding may provoke enquiries about the reasons, leading to unwanted speculation about (or even disclosure of) the mother's HIV status. Where such concerns arise, advice and support should be available from midwives and others involved in care.

See BHIVA (2010)
*Position statement
on infant feeding in
the UK* at
www.bhiva.org or
www.chiva.org.uk

In the rare instances where a mother with HIV who is on effective ART with a repeatedly undetectable viral load chooses to breastfeed, the British HIV Association (BHIVA) and the Children's HIV Association (CHIVA) no longer consider this as grounds for automatic referral to child protection teams. However, intensive support and monitoring of mother and baby are recommended.

Asylum seekers

Asylum seekers identified as HIV-positive (commonly through antenatal screening) face particular financial difficulties. Asylum support regulations allow a payment of £3 to be made for children up to three (£5 for under-ones) who are being supported by the UK Border Agency to help with the purchase of healthy foods. Pregnant women who are being supported by the UK Border Agency can also receive £3 a week under this scheme for the duration of their pregnancy.

Mental health

Mental health problems are more common in people with HIV than in the general population. This is probably for two reasons. Firstly, those with pre-existing mental health problems are often more vulnerable and may have been prone to engaging in high-risk sex or injecting drugs in the past. Secondly, those diagnosed with HIV still face stigma, isolation and discrimination, all of which may make them more likely to become depressed or anxious.

Many of those diagnosed with HIV in the 1980s and 90s stopped work and expected to become more unwell and die. While they later benefitted from improved treatments, which dramatically extended their prognosis, many had given up careers, cashed in pensions and life assurance policies and, after years out of the workplace, now face unemployment, dependence on state benefits and chronic ill-health. They may have experienced previous multiple bereavements and be vulnerable to depression. In general, HIV services in larger urban areas have access to psychiatrists and psychologists who specialise in this area. For the GP, management of mental health problems should be as normal.

case study

A long-term survivor

Andy is a 53-year-old gay man who has been living with HIV since 1989. He has a previous diagnosis of PCP and CMV retinitis and is visually impaired from this. He had a successful career, but when he became unwell with AIDS he gave up his job and has not worked since. He has a long antiretroviral history and has suffered from many side-effects over the years including renal stones and renal impairment from indinavir, marked lipoatrophy and lipodystrophy, which he found very stigmatising, and problematic GI side-effects which he has to manage symptomatically. He is currently stable on a complex ART regimen with an undetectable viral load and a CD4 count of 367/µl. He has multiple drug resistance because of his long antiretroviral history and has limited antiviral options at present. He is also on medication for raised cholesterol and hypertension, and he has impaired glucose tolerance. He is therefore taking an increasing list of non-HIV medication as well.

He suffered multiple bereavements in the 1980s losing many friends and his partner to AIDS. His family are aware of his HIV diagnosis, but live a long way from him; he has few friends and is very isolated due to his chronic ill health and inability to work. He has had several significant episodes of depression since being diagnosed with HIV. He feels quite bleak and negative about his future and his depression responds in part to SSRIs. He has made attempts to get back into employment, but is hampered by his poor vision and lack of work throughout the1990s. He presents a challenge on many levels to his GP, with whom he has a good relationship and whom he sees frequently.

> He presents a challenge on many levels to his GP, with whom he has a good relationship and whom he sees frequently.

Learning points

- The mental health problems experienced by people with HIV are similar to those seen in people coping with a range of chronic conditions or disabilities.
- Management of mental health problems is as normal in general practice, with the proviso that prescribed medications need to be checked for interactions with ART.

Remember that in your practice population, some people with mental health problems may be at increased risk from HIV and may not have been offered testing. Consider taking the opportunity in a review consultation to discuss this with them.

Clinical care for people with HIV

Managing HIV-related problems

1. The GP's role

For more, see BHIVA (2007) *Standards for HIV Clinical Care* at www.bhiva.org

In many ways, looking after someone with HIV is no different from looking after those with other chronic conditions. The specialist centres are responsible for initiating and monitoring ART and they remain responsible for prescribing it. The role of the GP may vary depending upon the health of the patient. In addition, the relationship the GP has with the patient, and the relationship between the patient and their specialist team, will affect how primary care is used. For many health problems, all that is needed is advice, reassurance or simple treatment. Nevertheless, there are times when immediate referral for assessment is likely to be appropriate.

It is important for GPs to have active communication with specialist HIV clinics. They should expect to be written to regularly, and should be prepared to notify specialists in return if there are significant changes in the patient's management or circumstances. It is also good practice to copy the HIV specialist into letters to/from other specialties as appropriate. Internal referrals from the HIV specialists should also be copied to the GP so that all clinicians are kept abreast of developments.

2. Health problems

See side effects of ART pages 71-74

Physical problems caused by HIV infection are significantly less common in the diagnosed patient now that ART is widely used. A patient with HIV who presents with symptoms might have:

- problems which relate to HIV disease (check the most recent CD4 count)
- side effects of ART
- an unconnected problem.

You may be able to take the first steps to distinguish which of these is the case. A recent CD4 count that is comfortably above 200 cells/µl makes HIV-related problems less likely. Check which antiretrovirals the patient is on, and check for side effects in the BNF section 5.3 and also on page 92.

3. Conditions that require urgent referral

For serious conditions associated with HIV see pages 29-35

Serious conditions due to HIV disease affect patients with CD4 counts below 200 cells/µl (except TB, see page 31).

Symptoms that require careful assessment include:
- respiratory
- visual (even if apparently minor, such as floaters)
- progressive or acute neurological problems.
    Side effects of ART are sometimes serious or even life-threatening – check which medication the patient is on.

4. Commoner conditions

For commoner conditions at a glance see pages 93-96

Many HIV-related problems are also common in patients who do not have HIV such as shingles and seborrhoeic dermatitis. Management of such conditions is generally the same and the GP is likely to be familiar with treatments. However, the immunosuppressed patient may require longer treatment than other patients.

5. Hepatitis B or C co-infection

For more, see BHIVA (2008) *Guidelines for the management of coinfection with HIV-1 and hepatitis B or C virus* at www.bhiva.org

Hepatitis B is common in those at risk from HIV. Chronic carriage is more frequent and may need treatment and monitoring in specialist clinics.

Hepatitis C was originally seen in those who were infected by shared needle use or contaminated blood products, but in recent years there has been an epidemic of hepatitis C amongst HIV-positive men who have sex with men (MSM). The route of transmission in most of these cases is unprotected sex rather than injecting drug use. Most HIV centres perform routine annual screening for hepatitis C as it can often be asymptomatic.

The HIV specialist team will manage any co-infected patients, but the primary care team can assist with adherence support and other medications to alleviate side effects of treatment such as antidepressants or sleeping tablets for those taking interferon/ribavirin for hepatitis C.

6. Managing patients with multiple co-morbidities

In general those infected with HIV have a higher risk of developing diseases associated with ageing, including cardiovascular disease (CVD), stroke, bone disease, chronic kidney disease (CKD) and a decline in cognitive function. The primary care team is well placed to manage and monitor such complex co-morbidities, but this is dependent on having a collaborative relationship with your patient and good communication with specialists.

Caring for people on antiretroviral therapy

Antiretroviral therapy (ART) has had an enormous impact on morbidity and mortality from HIV disease. Your patient (particularly if recently infected) has a good chance of living with their HIV for decades.

The management of HIV infection is complex and is undertaken by the specialist team.

Further information can be found on the BHIVA website.

For more, see BHIVA (2008) *Guidelines for the treatment of HIV-1 infected adults with antiretroviral therapy* at www.bhiva.org

1. How the drugs act

Entry inhibitors (EIs)

EIs prevent the viral membrane of HIV fusing with the target cell membrane and entering the cell.

Nucleoside/tide reverse transcriptase inhibitors (NRTIs)

NRTIs inhibit the enzyme reverse transcriptase that is key to transcribing the viral RNA into proviral DNA.

Non-nucleoside reverse transcriptase inhibitors (NNRTIs)

NNRTIs also inhibit the enzyme reverse transcriptase.

Integrase inhibitors (IIs)

IIs block the action of integrase, a viral enzyme that inserts the viral genome into the DNA of the host cell.

Protease inhibitors (PIs)

PIs inhibit the production of protease. Viral protease is needed to form new mature virus particles.

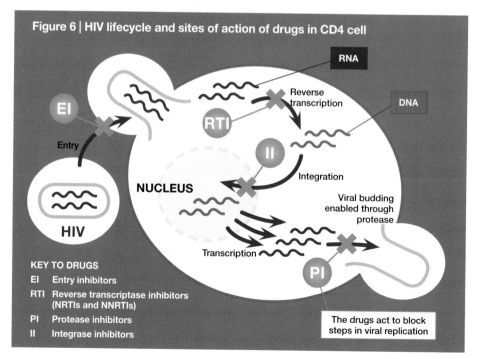

Figure 6 | HIV lifecycle and sites of action of drugs in CD4 cell

RNA

Reverse transcription

DNA

EI

RTI

Entry

II

Integration

NUCLEUS

Viral budding enabled through protease

HIV

Transcription

PI

KEY TO DRUGS
EI　Entry inhibitors
RTI　Reverse transcriptase inhibitors (NRTIs and NNRTIs)
PI　Protease inhibitors
II　Integrase inhibitors

The drugs act to block steps in viral replication

2. Drug combinations used in ART

For a list of drugs see page 91

HIV readily mutates in the process of replication. This means that resistance to single anti-HIV drugs develops very readily. For this reason drugs are generally used in combinations of three or more.

For initial regimens, a combination of two NRTIs with one NNRTI – now combined in a single tablet taken once a day – is often used. However, some people may be taking two NRTIs and a protease inhibitor (PI) boosted with a small dose of ritonavir (another PI) while other patients may be taking drugs from several classes. The choice of regimen will depend upon the need to minimise side effects and long-term toxicity, while providing an effective combination likely to suppress the virus long-term and be convenient for the patient. There are trials now looking at ways to reduce the number of drugs while maintaining optimal treatment outcomes. PI monotherapy has been shown to be appropriate for some individuals who are stable with an undetectable viral load.

3. When to start antiretroviral therapy

HIV specialists will take into account a number of factors when deciding when to start ART, including the CD4 count and risk of disease progression.

The choice of drugs will be informed by:
- knowledge of effectiveness of combination
- likelihood of resistance developing to chosen drug
- transmitted drug resistance (if there was evidence that the patient was infected by a strain of virus already showing resistance)
- drug toxicity
- pill burden
- drug-drug interactions
- and, increasingly, cost.

It may take some time for a drug regimen to be found that suits the patient. Because some drugs can have significant side effects, treatment centres tend to monitor patients more closely for the first six to eight weeks of therapy. The indications for commencing treatment and the recommended regimens have changed over time. National guidelines are regularly updated.

4. Monitoring progress

Monitoring of ART is primarily by viral load (see page 18). The aim is to reduce the viral load to undetectable levels, usually within three to six months of starting therapy.

5. Drug resistance

Resistance of the virus to ART is minimised if combination therapy is maintained at therapeutic levels in the blood stream. Any interference with its action (for example, through drug interactions) or with its administration (for example, through not adhering to prescribed regimens) can lead to resistance developing. Drug resistance, once established, is irreversible. Cross-resistance between classes of drugs means treatment choices are further limited.

Current guidelines recommend resistance testing at the time of diagnosis in order to check for transmitted drug resistant virus, as well as for those receiving ART in whom the viral load starts to rise. This allows the HIV-specialist to determine the most appropriate drug choice for the patient.

6. Adherence to antiretroviral therapy regimens

If people with hypertension miss their medication for a short period of time, it will still be effective when they re-start. Unfortunately this is not always the case with ART due to viral resistance. Adherence to a long-term drug regimen is one of the biggest challenges to those who live with HIV as well as to those who support them.

> **IMPORTANT!**
> Adherence is essential to prevent drug resistance developing.

Monitoring adherence is something the primary care team can do well. When the patient is seen, the GP or practice nurse should assess and monitor how they are coping with taking their medication and whether they are missing doses. Patients need to understand the reasons behind the requirement for optimal adherence as well as the possible consequences of missed doses. If they discontinue or repeatedly miss doses, try to explore the reasons for this.

Some once-a-day HIV combination therapies have a long half-life so there is some flexibility for stable patients with undetectable viral loads, meaning that timing does not have to be so strict. However, for these combinations missing doses altogether can lead to resistance and increases the risk of treatment failure.

The timing of the medication through the day may be complex, especially if medications for other conditions are included alongside the ART. A patient might be on one drug that must be taken some time before meals, but another that must be taken directly after. Even without these practical complications, it is hard to sustain a regular regimen without losing motivation or even simply forgetting doses. In some areas HIV specialists can arrange adherence support.

7. Drug interactions

PIs and NNRTIs are the groups most affected by drug interactions, being metabolised via the cytochrome P450 enzyme system in the liver. These interactions can lead to both increased toxicity and decreased efficacy. Dietary substances, herbal remedies and recreational drugs can all interact significantly.

> Check for drug interactions at:
> www.hiv-druginteractions.org

For further information see www.hiv-druginteractions.org. This site is run by the University of Liverpool and includes information on interactions between all the ART drug classes and most commonly prescribed medications, as well as dietary substances (under herbals/supplements/ vitamins) and recreational drugs (under illicit/recreational). There is an option to get individual queries answered by the team at Liverpool University. In some areas advice from specialist pharmacists linked to hospital HIV services is available.

8. ART side effects

While the benefits of ART are enormous, side effects are common and some may be serious. The specialist unit will be monitoring patients for side effects and most of them will be managed there. However, you may need to be aware of them in the event that an HIV patient attends general practice in an emergency, or uses the out-of-hours service. As antiretrovirals should not be stopped without good reason, management should always be discussed with a specialist before action is taken.

For ART side effects at a glance see page 92

Side effects are most common with the three older drug classes, NRTIs, NNRTIs and PIs. There is limited knowledge of the side effects of entry and integrase inhibitors at the time of writing as these are the newest classes of antiretrovirals. However, they appear to have a lower side effect profile than the other drugs.

For a full list of both serious and minor side effects, see the BNF section 5.3. See 'Quick reference' page 91 to identify which group each drug is in and page 92 for a table of side effects by drug type.

Minor side effects

Check for side effects at www.bnf.org section 5.3

ART can cause a huge range of minor side effects, which are generally listed in the BNF (section 5.3). The GP will often be able to manage minor side effects in the normal way. However, they should always check for drug interactions (see page 70). Symptomatic treatment is given on pages 93-96 (a guide to managing HIV-related problems).

Serious or unusual side effects

Some of the more serious side effects may not be the type of problem that GPs would normally consider could be due to medication. In addition, some serious 'unusual' side effects of ART can present in an insidious way, leaving the GP at risk of overlooking their significance.

Hypersensitivity

Hypersensitivity can occur with all drugs to different degrees. Abacavir and nevirapine are more often associated with serious reactions.

Abacavir. This is thought to occur in 8 per cent of those who take abacavir. Most HIV centres now perform Human Leukocyte Antigen (HLA) testing as this can help identify those more at risk from this reaction. However, a negative test does not mean there is no risk, only that it is less likely. It usually occurs within first six weeks, but not exclusively and can be life-threatening. It typically causes fever or rash but may cause a range of non specific symptoms such as fever, vomiting or myalgia. Seek advice urgently if suspected.

Nevirapine. Usually within the first four weeks, but not exclusively. Can be life-threatening. Typically causes rash and Stevens Johnson-type syndrome. This is more common at CD4 counts above 250 in women and 400 in men.

Psychiatric problems
Efavirenz is the drug most associated with this group of side effects and is commonly used as part of ART regimes. Nightmares, sleep disturbances, mood changes, behaviour changes and vivid (life-like) dreams are common. This is generally transient at the initiation of therapy but can be longstanding.

Hyperlipidaemia
The majority of ART drugs are implicated, with some less problematic than others. Increases are most likely when PIs are boosted with ritonavir.

ART can raise cholesterol and triglyceride levels, sometimes to an alarming degree. Diet can control levels in some, but those with high levels are increasingly treated with statins (atorvastatin, pravastatin) and fibrates (bezafibrate). Care must be taken when selecting such drugs due to interactions and hepatic metabolism. In particular, simvastatin, which is commonly prescribed in primary care, must be avoided in those on ART due to interactions. It is also essential to pay attention to other traditional CVD risk factors such as hypertension and smoking. Specialists should monitor lipids routinely.

IMPORTANT!
Consider hepatic metabolism and interactions when selecting drugs, especially statins.
Simvastatin is CONTRAINDICATED with antiretroviral therapy!

Lipodystrophy and lipoatrophy
First described with PIs, but may be associated with most antiretrovirals. Lipodystophy is a syndrome caused by ART in which there are changes in the distribution of body fat. Some individuals experience a loss of subcutaneous fat causing facial (particularly cheek and temple) thinning and limb and buttock wasting, known as lipoatrophy. It is particularly associated with NRTIs. Others develop central (truncal) adiposity with an increase in intra-abdominal fat, buffalo hump and breast enlargement. This is predominantly associated with PIs.

These two forms of lipodystrophy may co-exist and may also be associated with other metabolic abnormalities such as diabetes (due to insulin resistance) and hyperlipidaemia.

Although the drugs that cause it are now used less frequently in the UK, lipodystrophy/lipoatrophy may be one of the biggest fears of patients taking antiretroviral combinations. It can be stigmatising and distressing, often resulting in low self-esteem, isolation and depression. Awareness of the possibility of lipodystrophy may be a reason for some patients avoiding medication, and for some it may significantly affect adherence. Treatment for this syndrome is still largely unsatisfactory. A number of specialist centres offer treatment with polylactic acid, a filling agent for facial wasting.

Diabetes (Type II)

For ART drugs by class see page 91

Susceptibility to diabetes – probably through insulin resistance – is associated with ART and this may be complicated if the patient is overweight. It can be managed in the usual way, but monitoring and additional medication may induce 'adherence fatigue' in some patients. This can impact on both HIV and diabetes. Again, it is important to pay

Left to right:

1. Lipoatrophy. One of the biggest fears of patients taking ART, this syndrome may also be associated with metabolic abnormalities such as diabetes and hyperlipidaemia.

2. Lipodystrophy. A syndrome probably caused by ART and characterised by redistribution of body fat.

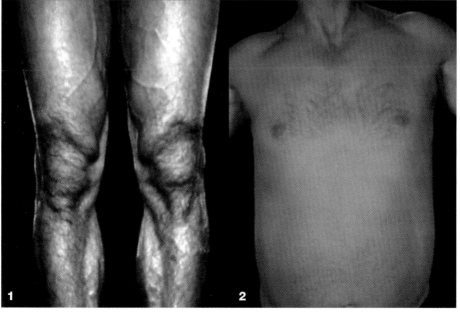

1 AND 2. MEDICAL ILLUSTRATION UK LTD

attention to other CVD risk factors in such patients. Diabetes may be associated with lipodystrophy (see above), but can also occur in patients on ART who do not have obvious lipodystrophy.

Renal problems

Tenofovir can be associated with a decline in renal function. This can be as serious as Fanconi's syndrome with renal tubular acidosis and glycosuria. A slow increase in serum creatinine, with a fall in eGRF and proteinuria can all mean the patient needs to switch off this drug. Specialist advice should be sought if this is suspected.

Ureteric colic, renal and ureteric stones

Atazanavir is the PI most commonly associated with these side effects, but others are also implicated, including indinavir although this is rarely used nowadays.

Lactic acidosis and hepatic toxicity

Probably caused by all NRTIs to varying degrees but mostly drugs such as didanosine and stavudine. These drugs are not commonly used in the UK now, but may have been used by patients from other parts of the world who have come to the UK. This potentially life threatening problem may present with non-specific symptoms such as nausea, loss of appetite or abdominal pain. In clear-cut cases patients will be obviously unwell – acidotic, hepatomegaly, with deranged liver function and raised serum lactate. Such patients need hospital admission and all ART medications are usually stopped.

Peripheral neuropathy

Mainly caused by didanosine and stavudine, less commonly lamivudine. Management of neuropathic pain generally consists of either tricyclic agents or anti-convulsants such as sodium valproate or gabapentin. Acupuncture can also be very helpful for some patients. Anaesthetic neuropathies are more difficult to manage and significant functional disability sometimes results.

Bone marrow suppression (anaemia, neutropenia)

Specialists will monitor this in patients on drugs that cause it; most commonly zidovudine, stavudine and lamivudine.

Pancreatitis

Most commonly caused by didanosine, but also stavudine, abacavir and lamivudine. Specialists will monitor amylase in patients on these drugs.

The dangers of being unaware of a patient's HIV treatment

The GP registrar at a large practice in inner London decided to carry out, with the PCT pharmacy advisor, a small study looking at how many patients could switch their lipid-lowering medication from more costly preparations to simvastatin. A search was carried out in late 2010 and a plan devised involving the patients.

Although most patients were happy to change, some were not and the change was not made. For three patients the registrar had to liaise with the hospital specialists about the best course of action (a cardiologist and a lipid-specialist).

Two patients who were taking atorvastatin and rosuvastatin respectively could not be contacted. Both patients (a middle-aged male and a young female) were HIV-positive and on antiretroviral therapy, including a protease inhibitor and a non-nucleoside inhibitor. They were looked after by different HIV-specialist centres in London. There had

been correspondence from their HIV-specialists in the past, but no letters had been received in the past year. In both cases there had been no detailed information about their lipid levels although the correspondence noted 'hyperlipidaemia'.

While the practice was some way from automatically switching these last two patients from their present statin to simvastatin it is not difficult to see how this might have happened if staff had not been aware of the patient's HIV status. The study was therefore discussed in the practice's thrice-yearly critical incident seminar since it provided important information and key learning.

Learning points:
- Simvastatin is contraindicated for patients on antiretroviral therapy as the risk of a serious adverse event from drug interaction is extremely high.
- Any proposed change to long-term therapy should always be discussed with the patient and hospital specialist.

Additional treatments for those with immunosuppression

Prophylaxis against opportunistic infections (OIs)

Pneumocystis pneumonia (PCP)

Patients who either have a CD4 count of less than 200 cells/µl or have already had an episode of PCP will be offered prophylaxis. Co-trimoxazole is the most effective agent, although drug reactions are seen commonly in the HIV-infected patient, so some may use dapsone or nebulised pentamidine. If the immune system recovers sufficiently following antiretroviral medication, this prophylaxis may be discontinued once the CD4 count is above 200 cells/µl and viral load is undetectable. Co-trimoxazole also protects against toxoplasmosis.

Mycobacterium avium intracellulare

Patients with a CD4 count of less than 50 cells/µl should be offered primary prophylaxis – usually azithromycin or rifabutin.

The patient who will not attend for specialist care

Some patients with HIV drift out of or reject specialist care. This is not as unlikely as it sounds. There are several reasons why this might happen including a bad experience at a particular specialist unit, adverse effects of ART, feeling better and believing treatment is no longer needed, overriding socio-economic or emotional problems, cultural or religious beliefs regarding disease causation and conventional medicine, or HIV-related stigma which in some communities is so pervasive that people may prefer to risk death than be seen coming out of an HIV clinic.

For more on stigma see page 81

If the GP has managed to keep a continuing relationship with the patient, this can be quite a stressful situation. The patient may not respond to discussion about the benefits of specialist care (with or without ART) and the need to attend. The GP should:

- try to maintain their relationship and contact with the patient – this is sometimes the most they can achieve for some time
- explore exactly what the patient's reasons are for not wishing to attend the HIV clinic – there may be a problem that can be addressed. In some areas there is more than one local HIV clinic to which the patient could be referred if there are concerns around confidentiality and being recognised
- continue to give gentle reminders to the patient of the health benefits of specialist care – whilst trying not to jeopardise the GP-patient relationship
- consider arranging (after discussion with the patient and the local lab) a CD4 count to assess how damaged their immunity is. With a high CD4 count the GP can be a bit more relaxed with the patient about the need for hospital review
- discuss the possibility of prophylactic treatments (such co-trimoxazole for PCP) with those that may not accept ART
- provide support to the patient's partner (if registered with you).

It is important to make sure you are fully aware of your responsibilities and what the GMC advises regarding patients who refuse specialist treatment. Always discuss with your practice team and also get advice about this from your medical defence union.

The dying patient

The advent of ART has meant that death as a result of HIV infection has become much less common. Usually it occurs in those who present with advanced disease or who are affected by other disease processes. Nevertheless, deaths still occur and the primary care team is likely to be involved in decisions regarding care as death approaches. With ART it is harder to define when a patient is terminally ill, because, given time, there can be recovery of immunity following changes in choice of antiretroviral. However, the patient remains vulnerable to overwhelming infection until that happens. With this uncertainty about outcome, there is a need to integrate palliative and curative approaches to care, and the goals of HIV palliative care need to be redefined.

1. Planning care and advance decisions

See BMA (2007) *Advance decisions and proxy decision-making in medical treatment and research* at www.bma.org.uk

Several life-threatening episodes may occur before the final terminal event. So, if not already addressed, planning should begin early on after immunity has started to deteriorate.

People with HIV commonly want to be in control of their care and treatment. All should be helped, if necessary, to express their requirements and preferences, which may change depending on the type of illness or stage of the condition. The desire for maximum patient choice in matters of care and treatment is nowhere more important than during episodes of acute, potentially life-threatening illness or when the patient is clearly approaching the terminal phase. Wherever possible, dying patients should be able to have partner, family, friends and people they trust around them, as well as appropriate medical, nursing and social care.

A well-planned death can also help those left behind to cope with their loss. In the UK, living wills or advance directives were largely developed by and for people with AIDS, though they are now used more widely. GPs may be asked to look at such documents, or contribute to their contents. In such circumstances it is always advisable to seek further advice and guidance, for example the BMA's ethical guidance.

2. Involvement of other healthcare professionals

Although the course of advanced HIV disease may be more 'up and down' than other conditions requiring palliative care, GPs should still be able to draw on their experience. Continuity and communication are extremely important in palliative care, and general practice is well-suited to providing these. The patient should be offered the support and involvement of palliative services and community nursing if appropriate. Some GPs can harness the support of specialist community nurses in HIV care. Hospice care may be needed. Respite care and symptom-control are currently the most important indications for admission.

3. Wills

People with deteriorating immunity should be advised to make a will as a matter of priority to avoid distressing disagreements and resentment after death. Civil partnership legislation provides full legal recognition for gay partners. However, regardless of civil partnership legislation, the will and testament is the document recognised by law and, if in doubt, patients should be advised to seek legal advice.

4. Death certification

See GMC (2009) *Confidentiality* at www.gmc-uk.org

The issue of death certification for people who have died of HIV-related illness can be complicated. It is commonly accepted that confidentiality persists after death and there are ethical considerations regarding such confidentiality when a patient or their relatives do not wish HIV to be recorded as a cause of death due to the stigma surrounding it. However, there is a clear legal requirement to indicate on the death certificate any underlying condition which may have contributed to a patient's death, and while this may potentially cause conflict with a patient's or their relatives' wishes, the clinician's duty to comply with the law is clear and unambiguous.

Until recently, in cases of HIV-related deaths, doctors have stated the obvious cause of death – for example, bronchopneumonia – but ensured that the box on the back of the certificate is ticked so that further information can be given at a later date. This has been crucial for the accuracy of national and regional statistical information. Increasingly, however, and in particular as a result of the Shipman Inquiry and the rise in deaths from hospital acquired infections, it has become clear that this area is under renewed scrutiny.

Section 4

HIV and the practice team

IN THIS SECTION

HIV and the practice team

There is a place for HIV prevention in the daily activities of the primary care team. Practice policies and systems, and appropriate training, can help to ensure that the patient with HIV receives high-quality care and staff are adequately prepared to provide this.

Sexual health promotion and HIV prevention in the practice

Growing concerns about the deterioration of sexual health in the UK is leading some practices to consider how they might play a part in promoting sexual health and reducing HIV transmission. For this role, clinical workers in primary care need both factual information and skills in sexual history taking and risk assessment.

> For more, see BASHH/ MedFASH (2010) *Standards for the management of sexually transmitted infections (STIs)* at www.bashh.org and www.medfash.org.uk

The British Association for Sexual Health and HIV and MedFASH have published *Standards for the management of sexually transmitted infections (STIs)* which provide clear guidance for all services that manage STIs. Standard 3, The clinical assessment, covers the need for appropriate history taking and Standard 2, Appropriately trained staff, covers competence and training.

Practice nurses and GPs have opportunities to:
* discuss and assess risk of having or acquiring HIV with individual patients
* promote safer sexual practices and condom use with those who are or may be at risk
* promote HIV testing when appropriate
* promote hepatitis B testing and immunisation when appropriate
* support harm minimisation with injecting drug users.

> For more, see Belfield T, Matthews P & Moss C (eds) (2011) *The handbook of sexual health in primary care*. London: FPA

Sexual health promotion interventions may occur during:
* travel advice consultations
* new patient checks
* contraceptive care
* cervical screening.

For more, see BASHH (2006) *UK Guideline for the use of post-exposure prophylaxis for HIV following sexual exposure* at www.bashh.org

Post-exposure prophylaxis following sexual exposure (PEPSE)

PEPSE is a course of ART offered to the uninfected sexual partner of someone known to have HIV in order to prevent infection after sex without a condom (or in the event of a condom rupturing). It is also sometimes offered to individuals who have had unprotected sex with someone from a high-risk group whose HIV status is unknown. Victims of sexual assault may also be offered PEPSE, depending on the risk assessment.

It is only recommended when the individual presents within 72 hours of exposure, and should be given as early as possible within this time frame.

PEPSE is available from HIV and GUM clinics and from Emergency Departments. Anyone presenting to primary care for PEPSE needs to be referred without delay to a specialist service where they can be assessed according to British Association for Sexual Health and HIV guidelines.

For more, see BASHH (2011) *UK National Guidelines on the Management of Adult and Adolescent Complainants of Sexual Assault* at www.bashh.org

Working with those with diverse needs

GPs are well placed to work with a wide range of people as they know their practice population well. It is well known that HIV can affect and infect anyone, but in the UK it is still most common in certain population groups. These are:

- men who have sex with men
- people from countries of high HIV prevalence especially Sub-Saharan Africa, but increasingly the Caribbean
- injecting drug users.

1. HIV stigma – a real issue

Members of all these groups may already feel marginalised or stigmatised in UK society and this can be exacerbated by the stigma and discrimination associated with HIV. Practitioners in primary healthcare need to be aware of some of the emotional and social pressures on these groups.

HIV infection is widely known to be incurable and people are afraid of contracting it. The link between sex or drug injecting and illness means that people who contract HIV are often thought to have brought it upon themselves as a result of personal irresponsibility or immorality. These factors combine to create a stigma that underpins prejudice, discrimination and even violence towards people with HIV. Negative attitudes to HIV are often reinforced in media coverage of the issue.

The impact of stigma

Stigma leads to some people not seeking HIV testing or being reluctant to agree to an HIV test, despite knowing they might be at risk. Others may not be aware that they could be infected, do not think that they belong to a group vulnerable to HIV, or may have little understanding about HIV transmission.

Few people with HIV feel able to be completely open about their status. A significant number do not tell employers or work colleagues or even close family members and friends. Some do not feel able to confide in their sexual partners or spouses for fear of rejection or abuse. The isolation and fear of being 'found out' and of possible rejection or discrimination, can lead to stress and depression.

Sometimes these fears are unfounded and confiding in trusted family members and friends can provide great support, but not always. Pregnant women have been subjected to physical violence, evicted from shared homes and ostracised by their communities when discovered to have HIV.

Support against stigma and discrimination

People with HIV are now covered from the point of diagnosis by the provisions of the Equality Act 2010. This offers protection against discrimination in a variety of fields, including employment and the provision of goods, facilities and services. Voluntary and community organisations which provide support and services for people with HIV have helped many to cope with both the medical and social consequences of a positive HIV diagnosis.

For more, see NAM (2006) *HIV and Stigma* at www.aidsmap.com

2. Men who have sex with men (MSM)

This term is used to include both men who identify as homosexual (and may call themselves gay) and those who have sexual encounters with other men without considering themselves to be homosexual. Gay men may have a sense of belonging and access to gay-oriented culture. However, other men who have sex with men often see themselves as bisexual or even heterosexual, are sometimes married, and may not be open about their same-sex encounters.

If a gay patient has a long-term partner, the practice can play a supporting role. Being registered with the same practice may make the partner's needs (for example, as a carer) easier to address. Civil partnerships provide same-sex couples with the same rights as married couples, including next-of-kin status.

3. Migrants from areas of high HIV prevalence

In the UK, people from Sub-Saharan Africa and parts of the Caribbean are known to be at higher risk of HIV infection. Communities from different parts of Africa and the Caribbean can be quite distinct in their culture and attitudes but HIV-related fear and prejudice are often very high, with resultant stigma and secrecy. Many people from high prevalence countries will know of family members or friends who have, or have died from, HIV. However, there is often a great reluctance to acknowledge this openly due to stigma. HIV may affect both parents as well as the children (infected or not), creating major family needs. Diagnosis in an adult should prompt consideration of possible infection in their children, who may have been born in a country not intervening to prevent mother-to-child transmission.

Cultural and religious beliefs may affect how people cope with a diagnosis of HIV and their beliefs about illness and treatment. It is important to present information in a culturally sensitive way and check patients' understanding – it has been known for people with limited English to hear 'the result is positive' as meaning that they are not infected with HIV. Beliefs should be explored in an open and non-judgemental manner, as they may affect future adherence to treatment. Have patient information leaflets about HIV available and give contact details of local support groups and HIV services. The GP's knowledge of the local community helps in providing a focus of care for families affected by HIV.

In many of the countries in these areas, attitudes to homosexuality are hostile and some have laws which criminalise sex between men. Men from these areas may therefore be less likely than those from the UK to disclose sexual activity with other men.

Some people with HIV are asylum seekers or refugees who have lost family members to violence and have fled their country. Some asylum seekers may ultimately be returned to countries where HIV treatment is unavailable to them.

Worries about employment, immigration or asylum can compound anxiety about confidentiality and disclosure of HIV status. When finding interpreters, it is important to be aware of HIV stigma and concerns about confidentiality within their community.

Figure 7 | Global prevalence of HIV 2009

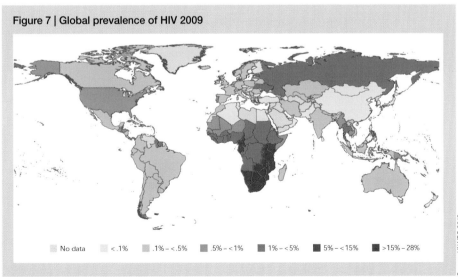

No data   <.1%   .1% – <.5%   .5% – <1%   1% – <5%   5% – <15%   >15% – 28%

Source: UNAIDS 2010

4. Injecting drug users

For more, see the Substance misuse management in general practice website (SMMGP), www.smmgp.org.uk

Those who have acquired HIV through injecting drugs (even if they no longer use them) may be aware of a double stigma – as drug users they are a socially excluded group, and this may be compounded by their HIV status. Those who have not wished, or been unable, to access support may be locked in a cycle of problems as they try to fund and feed their drug use. Dependent drug use may restrict the ability to attend appointments or take medication regularly. For some, HIV may not be a priority in the face of the daily problems associated with drug dependence. Low self-esteem, being in prison, previous abuse and other psycho-emotional problems may be underlying issues.

GPs involved in appropriate substitute prescribing in primary care will be aware of the benefits of this for the patient, in terms of harm reduction and access to healthcare. Do not assume that all injecting drug users are fully aware of the risks of sharing equipment or using non-sterile needles. It does no harm to repeat and reinforce the message.

5. Support organisations

There may be organisations offering support to MSM, Africans or other migrants with HIV infection in your area – your patient may (or may not) wish to be put in touch. Local organisations offering support to drug users may provide specific services for those with or at risk of HIV.

Practice policies and systems

1. Ensuring confidentiality and avoiding discrimination

Some patients with HIV perceive negative attitudes towards them from some GPs and health centres. Many have fears relating to confidentiality, especially around sensitive information such as HIV status, sexual orientation or lifestyle. Fear of breach of confidentiality is one of the main reasons patients with HIV cite when deciding whether or not to allow the hospital to communicate with their GP.

Developing a practice that is alive to patient concerns about confidentiality and fears of discrimination will support:
- open discussion of, and testing for, HIV with those who may be at risk
- disclosure of HIV status by those who already know they are infected
- open discussion about safer sexual and injecting practices
- improved quality of care for people with HIV infection.

Several studies have shown that the following interventions help in allaying the fears of patients:

- ensuring that your practitioners and clinicians are non-judgmental and empathic to different lifestyles. Consider in-house training for the team
- developing and implementing a non-discrimination policy with your practice – then displaying it to your patients
- developing and implementing an appropriate confidentiality statement – then displaying it to your patients.

(There are examples of these in the Sexual Health module of the e-GP programme – see page 102 for details.)

Practices which gain a reputation for being 'HIV-friendly' may see an increase in registrations from people with HIV as they exercise their right to choose their GP and 'shop around' to find the right practice.

2. Systems and record keeping

To support HIV testing

There are different systems to support HIV testing in the practice:

For aide-memoire
see page 90

- a pro forma record sheet or computer template can be used to collect data on individuals having an HIV test
- an aide-memoire (computer or paper-based) may help ensure that all issues are covered.

The contents of a pro forma should be discussed and agreed with clinical team members – there is a potential that highly confidential information of little value to future care may be unnecessarily recorded. If items are excluded for this reason then an aide-memoire or checklist may be needed. It does not record individual patient information.

For the patient with HIV

Some patients will be anxious about how their HIV status is to be recorded in the practice. It is best to raise the subject so this issue can be addressed and the benefits outlined (as well as the risks if the diagnosis is not clearly recorded).

Coding HIV infection

Computer systems have different options for coding HIV infection. Computer screens should not be visible to patients, although this may be difficult to achieve in a small consulting room. If screens are visible, the visibility of what is recorded should be considered, noting the fact that the patient may be accompanied when not consulting for an HIV-related problem. The practice will need to be able to search for patients with HIV infection in order, for example, to invite them for flu immunisation or to invite women for annual smears.

Records to support clinical care

The success of practice systems depends on reliable and rapid communication to and from the hospital each time the patient has attended and also when significant test results become available. If the patient is keen for you to be kept updated, ask them to emphasise this to their consultant. You can also write to the patient's HIV specialist asking for regular updates.

Records of antiretroviral and other drugs

Even if drugs are prescribed solely by the hospital, a clear record should be kept. On some practice computer systems it is possible to keep a record of drugs prescribed 'outside', which is the safest option as long as each and every hospital letter is checked for medication changes.

Records of CD4 count and viral load

Computer systems enable a simple template to be set up for use with patients with HIV. The most recent blood results can then be entered when they are made available by the hospital.

Review date

A review date system can act as a reminder to check that records are up to date. It is better to spend time chasing an absent CD4 result before you are faced with a patient with a bad cough.

3. Health and safety

Hepatitis B immunisation

The practice should have a system to ensure that staff who handle clinical specimens are immune to hepatitis B.

Prevention of needlestick injuries

Universal precautions in handling sharp instruments and body fluids are essential to reduce the risk of contracting HIV or other blood-borne viral infections in the healthcare setting. Approved sterilisation procedures and adequate disposal of sharp instruments are crucial components of this process. It is easy to forget the number of undiagnosed blood-borne infections, so it is essential to assume that all patients are potentially infected.

IMPORTANT!
A 'high risk' needlestick injury requires rapid and decisive action. Ensure all team members are aware of the practice policy on PEP.

Management of needlestick injuries

A 'high risk' needlestick injury requires rapid and decisive action if post-exposure prophylaxis (PEP) is to be given in time. This should be as soon as possible after the injury (within hours) to maximise effectiveness.

Post-exposure prophylaxis for occupational exposure

Discuss, develop and implement a practice policy on PEP with guidance from local occupational health and/or virology and ensure all team members are aware of its existence.

PEP policies in primary care should:
- advise how to manage the wound
- make clear the urgency and limited window of opportunity
- clarify who should be contacted for advice in your locality and how, including out of hours
- refer to locally agreed protocols for provision of PEP
- take into account other blood-borne viruses such as hepatitis B and C
- be adopted only in association with discussion and training.

PEP starter packs are usually held in the local hospital and, given the urgency, it is customary for PEP to be started and a thorough risk assessment to be made later. This allows for discontinuation where appropriate. It is not good practice for the affected healthcare worker to organise their own care in this situation.

The HIV-infected healthcare worker

The majority of procedures carried out in the primary care setting (assuming appropriate infection control procedures) pose no risk of transmission of HIV from healthcare worker to patient. Employing people infected with HIV is generally not a risk except in certain very specific situations where patients' tissues might be exposed to a carer's blood following injury ('exposure prone procedures').

See Department of Health (2005) *HIV-Infected Health Care Workers Guidance on Management and Patient Notification* at www.dh.gov.uk

However, the Department of Health requires all healthcare workers who are infected with HIV to seek appropriate expert medical and occupational health advice, and this should include how to modify or limit their work practices to avoid exposure prone procedures. HIV-infected healthcare workers must not rely on their own assessment of the risk they pose to patients.

Department of Health guidance for England and Wales on health clearance for TB, hepatitis B, hepatitis C and HIV requires all new healthcare workers who will perform exposure prone procedures to have health checks to establish that they are free from HIV infection before appointment. Parallel guidance applies in Scotland and Northern Ireland. Responsibility for ensuring this in general practice is assigned to GP principals.

See Department of Health (2007) *Health clearance for tuberculosis, hepatitis B, hepatitis C and HIV: New healthcare workers* at www.dh.gov.uk

While protecting the health and safety of patients, the right to confidentiality of staff and colleagues must be respected. Employers should assure infected healthcare workers that their status and rights as employees will be safeguarded so far as is practicable.

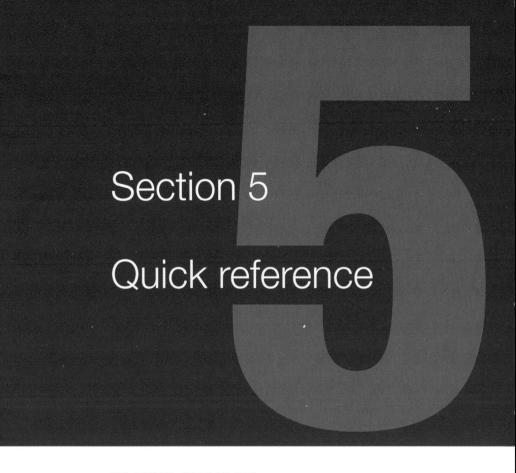

Section 5

Quick reference

IN THIS SECTION

Quick reference

HIV testing aide-memoire

Essentials
Make sure you explain:
- the benefits of testing and medical advantages of knowing one's HIV status
- how the patient will get the result.

Check their contact details
- Have you arranged an appointment for the result to be given to the patient?

Has the patient given clear consent to an HIV (or other) test?

Other areas to consider if needed
Does the patient understand:
- how HIV is transmitted?
- the difference between HIV and AIDS?
- the significance of the window period and the possible need for a repeat test?

Discussion of risk
- Risk to date
- Future risk/risk reduction

Discussion of implications of positive result

Discussion of implications of negative result
(ie as a wake-up call to change any risky behaviour)

Confidentiality

Coping with the wait
- Who knows they are having the test?
- Who is it safe to tell?

Ask the patient not to drink alcohol or take recreational drugs on day of result

Other useful points to consider

- Is there any written information that should be given to the patient?
- Is the test best done in primary care?
- Should there be any associated tests (eg hepatitis B and C, syphilis)?
- Is a repeat test required to cover the window period?
- Does the patient have a supply of appropriate condoms/lubricant?

Antiretrovirals by group

This list was correct at the time of writing. Up-to-date lists of agents are available on the following websites: www.bhiva.org, www.bnf.org, and www.hiv-druginteractions.org

Current antiretroviral drugs				
Nucleoside/tide reverse transcriptase inhibitors (NRTIs)	Non-nucleoside reverse transcriptase inhibitors (NNRTIs)	Protease inhibitors (PIs)	Entry inhibitors (EIs)	Integrase inhibitors (IIs)
abacavir	efavirenz	atazanavir	enfuvirtide (T-20)	raltegravir
didanosine (ddl)*	etravirine	darunavir	maraviroc	
emtricitabine (FTC)	nevirapine	fosamprenavir		
lamivudine (3TC)		indinavir*		
stavudine (d4T)*		lopinavir		
tenofovir		nelfinavir*		
zidovudine (AZT)		ritonavir		
		saquinavir		
		tipranavir		

*Rarely used in the UK.

Tablets containing more than one drug	
Trade name	Contains
Atripla	efavirenz, tenofovir, emtricitabine
Combivir	lamivudine, zidovudine
Kaletra	lopinavir, ritonavir
Kivexa	abacavir, lamivudine
Trizivir	abacavir, lamivudine, zidovudine
Truvada	tenofovir, emtricitabine

Trade names are not often used in the UK for single drug tablets. They are used more commonly for combination tablets which are listed above. Trade names are all given in the BNF.

Drug interactions – further information

Either

Check which ART class or group the antiretrovirals in question belong to (see table above).
Then check www.hiv-druginteractions.org
Or
Use the most recent BNF – section 5.3 – www.bnf.org

Drug side effects

Side effect	NRTI	NNRTI	PI
Hypersensitivity	abacavir	nevirapine	
Psychiatric problems		efavirenz	
Hyperlipidaemia	possibly all	possibly all	possibly all
Lipoatrophy/Lipodystrophy	possibly all	possibly all	possibly all
Diabetes (Type II)	possibly all	possibly all	possibly all
Renal problems	tenofovir		
Ureteric colic, renal and uteric stones			atazanavir indinavir
Lactic acidosis and hepatic toxicity	probably all especially didanosine stavudine		
Peripheral neuropathy	didanosine stavudine lamivudine (rare)		
Bone marrow suppression	zidovudine stavudine lamivudine		
Pancreatitis	didanosine stavudine (rare) abacavir (rare) lamivudine (rare)		

NB: there is limited knowledge of the side effects of entry and integrase inhibitors at the time of writing as these are the newest classes of antiretrovirals. However, they appear to have a lower side effect profile than the other drugs.

A guide to managing HIV-related problems

A patient with HIV who presents with symptoms might have:
- problems which relate to HIV disease (check the most recent CD4 count)
- side effects of ART
- an unconnected problem.

Patients who have developed symptoms which relate to HIV disease might have stopped taking their medication (ask) or might have developed resistance to their ART regimen. Current CD4 counts and viral load will clarify.

For patients who have not started ART, most of the problems mentioned below will improve, become less severe and rarely occur once they are established on ART.

It is important to be aware of possible ART interactions with oral medication, see www.hiv-druginteractions.org

Constitutional symptoms		
Condition	Notes	Management
Night sweats	Exclude serious causes, eg lymphoma, TB, chronic gut infection.	Supportive management.
Fatigue	Exclude serious causes eg tumour or opportunistic infections. Exclude common causes: • anaemia • thyroid deficiency • vitamin B deficiency • testosterone deficiency. Test for calcium, renal function. TFTs, FBC in all. Consider ART side effects.	May be managed in secondary or primary care, depending on cause. Testosterone replacement sometimes used if deficiency confirmed, seek specialist advice.
Weight loss	Exclude serious causes (tumour, chronic infection, opportunistic infections).	Dietary supplementation may have a role if all potentially serious causes have been excluded.

Skin conditions		
Condition	Notes	Management
Fungal infections		Generally respond to topical antifungals (often combined with topical steroids). Prolonged or repeated treatment may be required. Oral antifungals may be indicated for some (esp. nail infections).
Herpes zoster Herpes simplex		Will respond to antivirals such as aciclovir but longer courses at higher doses may be needed. Long-term use of antivirals is helpful if the problem is recurrent.
Warts *Molluscum contagiosum*		Topical imiquimod or podophyllotoxin. Cryotherapy.
Bacterial infections eg impetigo folliculitis		Oral antibiotics are more effective and less likely to be associated with resistance than topical antibiotics.
Seborrhoeic dermatitis		Topical antifungal and hydrocortisone combinations. Antifungal shampoos often helpful.
Psoriasis		Usual management, but may be much less responsive.
Kaposi's sarcoma		Will require specialist treatment.

The mouth		
Condition	Notes	Management
Oral candida	Can cause significant discomfort and difficulty in eating/drinking.	Systemic anti-fungal agents are effective. If recurrent can indicate poor immune function and need for specialist opinion. Long-term use of antifungals occasionally indicated if the problem is recurrent. May need referral if severe or resistant infection.
Aphthous ulceration		Topical oral steroid creams. Specialists use thalidomide if troublesome.
Oral hairy leukoplakia		Generally asymptomatic and does not require treatment.
Gingivitis	Maintaining good oral hygiene and dental care is important for all immunocompromised patients.	Chlorhexidine mouth washes. Oral metronidazole. Referral to dentist.
Kaposi's sarcoma		Requires specialist treatment. May disappear with effective ART.
Dental abscess		Oral antibiotics. Referral to dentist.

The rest of the gastrointestinal tract

Condition	Notes	Management
Nausea	May be caused by ART.	Managed with either a dopaminergic agent (metoclopramide or domperidone) or agents such as levomepromazine.
Oesophageal candida	Indicates severe immunosuppression.	As for oral candida (see The mouth above) but generally managed by specialists or GPwSI as usually diagnosed at endoscopy.
Diarrhoea	Possible causes: • side effect of ART • pancreatic insufficiency • HIV in the intestinal mucosa • intestinal pathogens Check if could be travel-related diarrhoea. Take stool samples. More likely to have lactose intolerance and remember coeliac too.	Loperamide for symptomatic treatment. Codeine is sometimes helpful. Salmonella and campylobacter respond to ciprofloxacin or macrolides as appropriate. Less common organisms such as *Cryptosporidium sp* and *Microsporidium* sp may be responsible if patient has had low CD4 count. Management should be guided by microscopy and culture results and information on drug interactions: seek specialist advice if necessary.

Respiratory conditions

Condition	Notes	Management
Chest infection	Exclude PCP (see pages 29-30). Exclude TB-like infections (see page 31).	Community-acquired chest infections should respond to first line antibiotics.

Neurological conditions – see also page 32 for serious conditions that require admission

Condition	Notes	Management
Peripheral neuropathy	May be caused by HIV or antiretrovirals.	Pain management similar to usual approaches to neuropathic pain. Gabapentin or other drugs used in neuralgia may help.

Genital conditions

Condition	Notes	Management
Genital candida		Topical or systemic antifungal agents (clotrimazole, fluconazole). Systemic antifungals are sometimes used long-term to prevent recurrence.
Genital herpes		Aciclovir – may be needed in longer courses and at a higher end of the dose range than usual. Long-term use of aciclovir or similar may be used to suppress frequent recurrences.
Genital and perianal warts		Frequently recurrent and more difficult to treat. Topical therapy (imiquimod or podophyllotoxin) or cryotherapy may help. Refer to GUM unless responding well to topical therapy. Anal intraepithelial neoplasms and anal squamous cell carcinomas are much more common in the HIV-positive population so referral for anoscopy is indicated if there are atypical features.

Sexual dysfunction

Condition	Notes	Management
Erectile dysfunction Loss of libido	May be multifactorial. HIV-related causes include: • effect of HIV • fear of transmitting infection • ART • vascular problems. In men check testosterone level.	Phosphodiesterase inhibitors can be used, but they interact with PIs and NNRTIs and expert advice should be sought. Testosterone replacement is sometimes used on specialist advice. There is increasing evidence that erectile dysfunction can predict underlying vascular problems and hence increased risk for CVD/IHD.

Psychological conditions

Condition	Notes	Management
Stress	Stress is common. May be exacerbated by stigma.	Supportive counselling and/or specialist or psychological support is sometimes necessary.
Depression Bipolar disorder	May be seen more commonly in people with HIV. Some antiretrovirals may be associated with psychiatric disturbance.	Beware drug interactions if considering antidepressants.
HIV-related brain impairment	Can cause functional impairment and lead to significant care needs.	Seek specialist advice. Consider needs of carer(s).

Visual problems

See page 33 for CMV retinitis, a serious condition that requires urgent referral to ophthalmology.

Information to support implementation of UK HIV testing guidelines

Clinical indicator diseases for HIV infection

The *UK National Guidelines for HIV Testing 2008* recommend offering an HIV test to every patient presenting with a clinical indicator disease for HIV infection. (See table for adults on following page.)

See www.bhiva.org

Clinical indicator diseases for paediatric HIV infection		
	AIDS-defining conditions	Other conditions where HIV testing should be considered
ENT		Chronic parotitis, Recurrent and/or troublesome ear infections
Oral		Recurrent oral candidiasis Poor dental hygiene
Respiratory	Pneumocystis CMV pneumonitis Tuberculosis	Recurrent bacterial pneumonia Lymphoid interstitial pneumonitis Bronchiectasis
Neurology	HIV encephalopathy meningitis/encephalitis	Developmental delay Childhood stroke
Dermatology	Kaposi's sarcoma	Severe or recalcitrant dermatitis Multidermatomal or recurrent herpes zoster Recurrent fungal infections Extensive warts or molluscum contagiosum
Gastroenterology	Wasting syndrome Persistent cryptosporidiosis	Unexplained persistent hepatosplenomegaly Hepatitis B infection Hepatitis C infection
Oncology	Lymphoma Kaposi's sarcoma	
Haematology		Any unexplained blood dyscrasia including: • thrombocytopenia • neutropenia • lymphopenia
Ophthalmology	Cytomegalovirus retinitis	Any unexplained retinopathy
Other	Recurrent bacterial infections (eg meningitis, sepsis, osteomyelitis, pneumonia etc) Pyrexia of unknown origin	

Source: UK National Guidelines for HIV Testing 2008

Clinical indicator diseases for adult HIV infection		
	AIDS-defining conditions	**Other conditions where HIV testing should be offered**
Respiratory	Tuberculosis Pneumocystis	Bacterial pneumonia Aspergillosis
Neurology	Cerebral toxoplasmosis Primary cerebral lymphoma Cryptococcal meningitis Progressive multifocal leucoencephalopathy	Aseptic meningitis/encephalitis Cerebral abscess Space occupying lesion of unknown cause Guillain-Barré Syndrome Transverse myelitis Peripheral neuropathy Dementia Leucoencephalopathy
Dermatology	Kaposi's sarcoma	Severe or recalcitrant seborrhoeic dermatitis Severe or recalcitrant psoriasis Multidermatomal or recurrent herpes zoster
Gastroenterology	Persistent cryptosporidiosis	Oral candidiasis Oral hairy leukoplakia Chronic diarrhoea of unknown cause Weight loss of unknown cause Salmonella, shigella or campylobacter Hepatitis B infection Hepatitis C infection
Oncology	Non-Hodgkin's lymphoma	Anal cancer or anal intraepithelial dysplasia Lung cancer Seminoma Head and neck cancer Hodgkin's lymphoma Castleman's disease
Gynaecology	Cervical cancer	Vaginal intraepithelial neoplasia Cervical intraepithelial neoplasia Grade 2 or above
Haematology		Any unexplained blood dyscrasia including: • thrombocytopenia • neutropenia • lymphopenia
Ophthalmology	Cytomegalovirus retinitis	Infective retinal diseases including herpesviruses and toxoplasma Any unexplained retinopathy
ENT		Lymphadenopathy of unknown cause Chronic parotitis Lymphoepithelial parotid cysts
Other		Mononucleosis-like syndrome (primary HIV infection) Pyrexia of unknown origin Any lymphadenopathy of unknown cause Any sexually transmitted infection

Source: UK National Guidelines for HIV Testing 2008

Local diagnosed HIV prevalence

The *UK National Guidelines for HIV Testing 2008* suggest an HIV test should be routinely offered as part of new patient checks in general practice, where local diagnosed HIV prevalence is over two per 1,000 population. A data table of diagnosed HIV prevalence for each PCT and local authority in England can be found on the 'HIV & STIs/data for commissioners' page of the HPA website (www.hpa.org.uk).

Figure 8 | HIV-infected individuals accessing HIV care by area of residence in 2009: Rate per 1,000 aged 15-59 years

More than 2 per 1,000
1 to 2 per 1,000
Less than 1 per 1,000

London

Source: Health Protection Agency

Useful sources for clinicians

Reference documents to bookmark or keep in the practice

Association of British Insurers & British Medical Association (2010) *Medical information and insurance. Joint guidelines from the British Medical Association and the Association of British Insurers.* London: British Medical Association. Available at www.bma.org.uk

Belfield T, Matthews P & Moss C (eds) (2011) *The handbook of sexual health in primary care.* London: FPA.

British Association for Sexual Health and HIV, British HIV Association, British Infection Society (2008) *UK National Guidelines for HIV Testing 2008.* Available at www.bhiva.org, www.bashh.org and www.britishinfection.org

British Association for Sexual Health and HIV and Medical Foundation for AIDS & Sexual Health (2010) *Standards for the management of sexually transmitted infections (STIs).* Available at www.bashh.org or www.medfash.org.uk

British HIV Association (2008) Guidelines for the immunization of HIV-infected adults. *HIV Med* **9**: 795-848. Available at www.bhiva.org

British HIV Association & Children's HIV Association (2008) *Guidelines for the management of HIV infection in pregnant women.* Available at www.bhiva.org

British National Formulary section 5.3. Available at www.bnf.org

Department of Health *Immunisation against infectious disease* ('The Green Book'). Updated regularly at www.dh.gov.uk

General Medical Council (2009) *Confidentiality.* London: General Medical Council. Available at www.gmc-uk.org

University of Liverpool HIV Pharmacology Group. Comprehensive listings of interactions between HIV drugs and others, including herbal medicines and recreational drugs. They will answer individual queries from doctors. Available at www.hiv-druginteractions.org

Organisations and websites

aidsmap
www.aidsmap.com
Extensive information on treatments, including updates on the latest research. Database of HIV organisations worldwide (including UK).

British Association for Sexual Health and HIV (BASHH)
www.bashh.org
Medical specialist society for professionals in GUM/HIV that produces clinical effectiveness guidelines for the management of STIs.

British HIV Association (BHIVA)
www.bhiva.org
Regularly updated guidelines for the treatment and care of HIV-infected adults including HIV testing, treatment with ART, HIV in pregnancy, HIV and hepatitis co-infection, immunisation, sexual and reproductive health, adherence support and management of other co-morbidities.

Children's HIV Association of the UK and Ireland (CHIVA)
www.chiva.org.uk
Articles and protocols on treatment and care of HIV-infected children and information on the Children's HIV National Network (CHINN).

Health Protection Agency (HPA)
www.hpa.org.uk
Up-to-date figures for HIV and other infections in the UK, including graphs and slides that can be downloaded.

NHS Evidence
www.evidence.nhs.uk
A wealth of journal papers guidelines and other useful information

Royal College of General Practitioners' Sex, Drugs and HIV Group
www.rcgp.org.uk/substance_misuse/sex__drugs_and_hiv_group.aspx
A special interest group concerned with education and policy. Organises national conferences.

Scottish HIV and AIDS Group (SHIVAG)
www.shivag.co.uk
Professional website with news, discussion forums and useful documents regarding HIV in Scotland.

Substance misuse management in general practice (SMMGP)

www.smmgp.org.uk
Organisation providing information and support to GPs prescribing for drug users. Produces a regular newsletter.

Professional development for clinicians on HIV and sexual health

Listed below are the most important CPD options for those interested in HIV and sexual health.

e-learning

This is a selection of e-learning specifically about HIV. HIV is also mentioned in modules about conditions associated with HIV, such as sexually transmitted infections, viral hepatitis and tuberculosis.

e-learning for healthcare sessions

http://e-lfh.org.uk/projects/egp
e-GP is RCGP education for GPs and practice nurses on topics within the GP curriculum. Relevant modules include:
GPS 11 001 Sexual Health – Indicators of Risk
GPS 11 002a The Sexual History – Sexual History Taking in the General Practice Context
GPS 11 002b The Sexual History – The Partner History
GPS 11 002c The Sexual History – Assessing Condom Use, Pregnancy Risk and Symptoms
GPS 11 014a HIV and Why Early Diagnosis Matters
GPS 11 014b HIV Indicator Conditions

http://e-lfh.org.uk/projects/hiv-sti
eHIV-STI has been developed by BASHH and the Federation of the Royal Colleges of Physicians for healthcare professionals treating and supporting people with sexually transmitted infections, including HIV. Relevant modules include:
HIV-STI 01 02 Sexual History
HIV-STI 11 01 HIV Testing
HIV-STI 11 03 HIV Disclosure and Partner Notification
HIV-STI 12 01 Natural History of HIV Infection
HIV-STI 12 07 Antiretroviral Side Effects and Toxicities

Royal College of General Practitioners Online Learning Environment
www.elearning.rcgp.org.uk
Sexual health in general practice
This e-module forms part of the Introductory Certificate in Sexual Health but can also be completed as a stand-alone. It covers HIV testing and diagnosis.

BMJ Learning
www.group.bmj.com/products/learning
Relevant modules are:
Testing for HIV in general practice in the UK
HIV infection: diagnostic picture tests

Face-to-face training

Introductory Certificate in Sexual Health (ICSH)
Royal College of General Practitioners
www.rcgp.org.uk/substance_misuse/sex__drugs_and_hiv_group/intro_cert_in_sexual_health.aspx
One-day educational event for GPs and practice nurses with no previous training in sexual health. A useful first step. Participants should complete the e-module 'Sexual health in general practice' before attending.

Sexually Transmitted Infections Foundation (STIF) course
British Association for Sexual Health and HIV
www.bashh.org/stif
Multidisciplinary training in the attitudes, skills and knowledge required for the prevention and management of STIs, including sexual history taking and HIV testing in non-GUM settings using a variety of educational techniques. The course comprises five to six hours of e-learning and one or two days of face-to-face training.

STIF competency
British Association for Sexual Health and HIV
www.bashh.org/stif_ic
A modular competency-based training and assessment package for non-specialist healthcare professionals requiring more specialist skills in STI management.

Useful sources for patients

Leaflets to have in the practice
HIV FPA
www.fpa.org.uk/professionals/publicationsandresources
An information leaflet about HIV and HIV testing for the general public.
Available free to general practices in England in multiples of 50 copies. In
the rest of the UK £7.50 per 50 copies.
To order, email allocations@fpa.org.uk
Downloadable pdf on the website.

Your Next Steps Terrence Higgins Trust
www.tht.org.uk/informationresources/publications
This booklet is for people who have just found out they have HIV.
Up to three copies free of charge, 35p per copy in bulk.
To order, call 0845 12 21 200 or online at the website.
Downloadable pdf on the website.

Other printed resources for people with HIV

NAM patient information booklets
www.aidsmap.com/resources/booklets
Plain English information on testing, treatment and living with HIV
(14 booklets).
Available free to people living with HIV. For organisations, £1 each.
To order, call 020 7840 0050, email info@nam.org.uk or online at the
website.
Downloadable pdfs on the website.

Terrence Higgins Trust *Living with HIV* booklet series
www.tht.org.uk/howwecanhelpyou/livingwithhiv
Information to enable people living with HIV to remain well informed and
positive about life.
Up to three copies free of charge, 35p per copy in bulk.
To order, call 0845 12 21 200 or online at the website.
Downloadable pdfs on the website.

Websites for HIV information

aidsmap
www.aidsmap.com
A wealth of easy-to-read information on HIV and ART. Some online
information resources available in French, Portuguese, Spanish,
Romanian and Russian.

AVERT (AIDS education and research)
www.avert.org
Abundant information on HIV-related education, prevention and care, including information for young people, statistics and information about transmission, treatment and testing.

HIV i-base
www.i-base.info
HIV information for healthcare professionals and HIV-positive people including information on HIV treatment guidelines, answers to HIV treatment questions and materials for advocacy.

National AIDS Trust
www.nat.org.uk
A national policy organisation. Useful information on legal and policy issues for people with HIV and professionals.

Terrence Higgins Trust
www.tht.org.uk
Sections of website for people with HIV and for others requiring sexual health information.

Organisations for support and information

You may well have local organisations working with people with HIV. Here we list just a few national organisations which may help you or your patient to identify local ones.

African AIDS Helpline
http://africaninengland.org.uk
0800 0967 500
Mon – Fri (except bank holidays), 10am – 6pm.
(Answerphone service available outside these hours.)
Languages available: English, French, Portuguese, Luganda, Shona and Swahili.

HIV Support Centre
www.thehivsupportcentre.org.uk
Provides support services and information in Northern Ireland.
Helpline: 0800 137 437

Positively UK (formerly Positively Women)
www.positivelyuk.org
A national charity championing the rights of people living with HIV.
People living with HIV answer the helpline and will ring back free of charge.
Helpline: 020 7713 0222
Mon – Fri, 10am – 5pm (Thurs until 8pm).

Sexual health information line
0800 567 123 (calls may be charged from mobile phones).
24-hour, free, confidential helpline for anyone concerned about HIV or
sexual health. Translation services available and can provide details of
local HIV organisations.

Terrence Higgins Trust
www.tht.org.uk
A large charitable organisation with services in many British towns and
cities. Produces a wide range of written resources on HIV prevention and
living with HIV.
THT Direct helpline: 0845 1221 200
Mon – Fri 10am – 10pm, Sat/Sun 12pm – 6pm.

Waverley Care
www.waverleycare.org
Charity providing support services and information in Scotland.
Information centre: 0131 661 0982

Bibliography

Association of British Insurers & British Medical Association (2010) *Medical information and insurance: joint guidelines from the British Medical Association and the Association of British Insurers*. Available at www.bma.org.uk (accessed 18 March 2011)

Belfield T, Matthews P & Moss C (eds) (2011) *The handbook of sexual health in primary care*. London: FPA.

British Association for Sexual Health and HIV (2010) *BASHH Statement on HIV window period* 15 March 2010. Available at www.bashh.org (accessed 14 January 2011)

British Association for Sexual Health and HIV (2010) *UK National Guidelines on the Management of Adult and Adolescent Complainants of Sexual Assault*. Available at www.bashh.org (accessed 14 January 2011)

British Association for Sexual Health and HIV (2006) *UK Guideline for the use of post-exposure prophylaxis for HIV following sexual exposure*. Available at www.bashh.org (accessed 14 January 2011)

British Association for Sexual Health and HIV, British HIV Association, British Infection Society (2008) *UK National Guidelines for HIV Testing 2008*. Available at www.bhiva.org, www.bashh.org and www.britishinfection.org (accessed 14 January 2011)

British Association for Sexual Health and HIV and Medical Foundation for AIDS & Sexual Health (2010) *Standards for the management of sexually transmitted infections (STIs)*. Available at www.bashh.org and www.medfash.org.uk (accessed 14 January 2011)

British Association for Sexual Health and HIV, British HIV Association, Faculty of Sexual and Reproductive Healthcare (2008) *UK guidelines for the management of sexual and reproductive health of people living with HIV infection*. Available at www.bhiva.org (accessed 14 January 2011)

British HIV Association (2008) *Guidelines for the immunization of HIV-infected adults*. Available at www.bhiva.org (accessed 14 January 2011)

British HIV Association (2008) *Guidelines for the management of coinfection with HIV-1 and hepatitis B or C virus.*
Available at www.bhiva.org (accessed 14 January 2011)

British HIV Association (2008) *Guidelines for the treatment of HIV-1 infected adults with antiretroviral therapy.*
Available at www.bhiva.org (accessed 14 January 2011)

British HIV Association, British Association for Sexual Health and HIV, British Infection Society, Royal College of Physicians (2007) *Standards for HIV Clinical Care.*
Available at www.bhiva.org (accessed 14 January 2011)

British HIV Association and Children's HIV Association (2008) Guidelines for the management of HIV infection in pregnant women. *HIV Med* **9**: 452-502.
Available at www.bhiva.org (accessed 14 January 2011)

British Medical Association (2007) *Advance decisions and proxy decision-making in medical treatment and research – guidance from the BMA's Medical Ethics Department.*
Available at www.bma.org.uk (accessed 14 January 2011)

Department of Health (2005) *HIV-infected health care workers: Guidance on management and patient notification.*
Available at www.dh.gov.uk (accessed 14 January 2011)

Department of Health (2007) *Health clearance for tuberculosis, hepatitis B, hepatitis C and HIV: New healthcare workers.*
Available at www.dh.gov.uk (accessed 14 January 2011)

Department of Health, Social Services and Public Safety of Northern Ireland (2009) *HIV-infected health care workers: Guidance on management and patient notification.*
Available at www.dhssps.gov.uk (accessed 27 February 2011)

Department of Health, Social Services and Public Safety of Northern Ireland (2009) *Health Clearance for Tuberculosis (TB), Hepatitis B, Hepatitis C and HIV: New Healthcare Workers with Direct Clinical Contact with Patients.*
Available at www.dhsspsni.gov.uk (accessed 18 March 2011)

Expert Advisory Group on AIDS (2006) *Oral sex and transmission of HIV – statement of risk.*
Available at www.dh.gov.uk (accessed 14 January 2011)

Faculty of Sexual and Reproductive Healthcare (2009) *UK Medical Eligibility Criteria for Contraceptive Use*. Available at www.fsrh.org (accessed 27 January 2011)

Faculty of Sexual and Reproductive Healthcare (2011) *Clinical Guidance: Drug Interactions with Hormonal Contraception.* Available at www.fsrh.org (accessed 14 January 2011)

General Medical Council (2009) *Confidentiality*. Available at www.gmc-uk.org (accessed 14 January 2011)

Health Protection Agency (2010) *HIV in the United Kingdom: 2010 Report*. Available at www.hpa.org.uk (accessed 14 January 2011)

Health Protection Agency (2010) *Time to test for HIV: expanded healthcare and community HIV testing in England*. Available at www.hpa.org.uk (accessed 14 January 2011)

Leake-Date H & Fisher M (2007) HIV Infection. In: Whittlesea C & Walker R (eds) *Clinical Pharmacy and Therapeutics* 4th Edition. Oxford: Churchill Livingstone.

NAM (2006) *HIV and stigma*. Available at www.aidsmap.com (accessed 14 January 2011)

Department of Health (2003) *Screening for infectious diseases in pregnancy: Standards to support the UK antenatal screening programme* Available at www.dh.gov.uk (accessed 18 March 2011)

Scottish Government (2005) *HIV-Infected Health Care Workers: Guidance on Management and Patient Notification.* Available at www.scotland.gov.uk (accessed 27 February 2011)

Scottish Government (2008) *Health Clearance for Tuberculosis, Hepatitis B, Hepatitis C and HIV for new Healthcare Workers with direct clinical contact with patients.* Available at www.scotland.gov.uk (accessed 18 March 2011)

Welsh Assembly Government (2005) *HIV-Infected Health Care Workers: guidance on management and patient notification.* Available www.wales.nhs.uk/documents (accessed 18 March 2011)

Section 6

Subject
index

Subject index

Notes: page numbers suffixed by 'f' indicate figures, by 'i' indicate images and by 't' indicate tables.

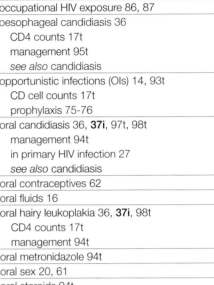